STECK-VAUGHN
CRITICAL THINKING

Reading, Thinking, and Reasoning Skills

Authors

Don Barnes
Professor of Education
Ball State University; Muncie, Indiana

Arlene Burgdorf
Former Resource Consultant
Hammond Indiana Public Schools

L. Stanley Wenck
Professor of Educational Psychology
Ball State University; Muncie, Indiana

Consultant

Gloria Sesso
Supervisor of Social Studies
Half Hollow Hills School District; Dix Hills, New York

LEVEL

A	B	C	D	E	F

STECK-VAUGHN
COMPANY
A Subsidiary of National Education Corporation

ACKNOWLEDGMENTS

Executive Editor
Elizabeth Strauss

Project Editor
Anita Arndt

Consulting Editor
Melinda Veatch

Design, Production, and Editorial Services
The Quarasan Group, Inc.

Contributing Writers
Tara McCarthy
Linda Ward Beech

Cover Design
Linda Adkins Graphic Design

Photography:
p. 5   — H. Armstrong Roberts
p. 27   — Nita Winter
p. 49   — Nita Winter
p. 69   — Kathy Sloane
p. 89   — Nita Winter
p. 109 — Kathy Sloane

Illustration:
pp. 7, 47, 114 — Linda Hawkins
pp. 9, 12, 16, 23, 31, 48, 67 — Lynn McClain
pp. 10, 14, 18, 24, 28, 30 — Kenneth Smith
pp. 25, 63, 72, 92 — Liz Allen
pp. 29, 40, 45, 53, 59, 73, 75, 117, 121, 126 — Scott Bieser
pp. 33, 34, 39, 51 — Ruth Brunke
pp. 35, 43, 57, 72, 83, 96, 103, 111, 118 — Charles Varner/Carol Bancroft & Friends
pp. 42, 54, 66, 79, 81, 84, 91 — Leslie Dunlap/Publishers Graphics
pp. 44, 50, 88, 97, 100, 104, 119 — Joel Snyder/Publishers Graphics
pp. 68, 70, 74, 87, 99, 113, 127 — Barbara Lanza/Carol Bancroft & Friends
pp. 80, 116, 124 — Jackie Rogers/Carol Bancroft & Friends

ISBN 0–8114–6602–7

TABLE OF CONTENTS

TABLE OF CONTENTS

Knowing

Knowing means getting the facts together. Let's try it out. Where do you think this photograph was taken? Are the three boys on the same team? How do you know? Why are they sitting on the bench? Is the ball in play now? How can you tell?

The words in each word web name things in a group. Choose a word from the box below that describes the group. Write the word to finish the web. The first one is done for you.

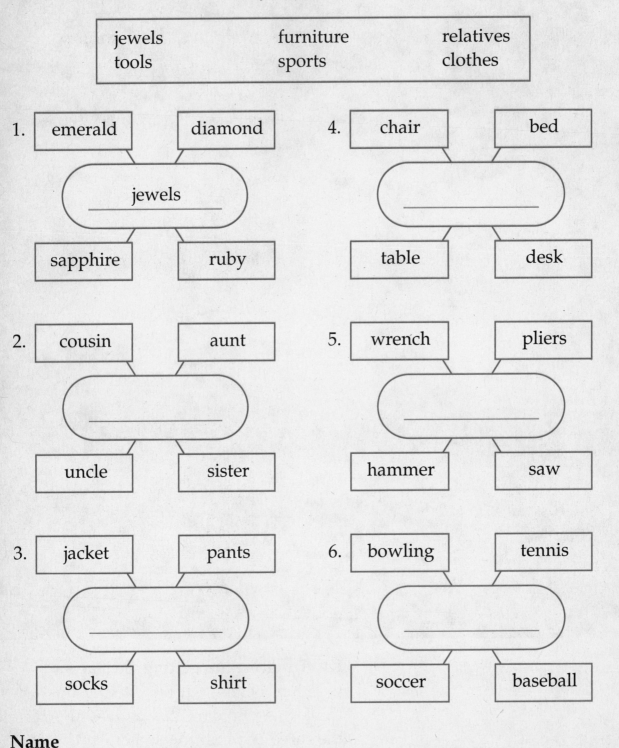

| jewels | furniture | relatives |
| tools | sports | clothes |

1. emerald · diamond · __jewels__ · sapphire · ruby

2. cousin · aunt · _____ · uncle · sister

3. jacket · pants · _____ · socks · shirt

4. chair · bed · _____ · table · desk

5. wrench · pliers · _____ · hammer · saw

6. bowling · tennis · _____ · soccer · baseball

Name _____

Critical Thinking, Level C © 1993 Steck-Vaughn

Imagine that you have four cookbooks about different foods. Next to each cookbook write the names of four foods that might be in that book's recipes. Use the food names in the box.

hot dogs	broccoli	apples	shrimp
turkey	potatoes	perch	tuna
peaches	salmon	watermelon	chicken
corn	cherries	beef	carrots

1.

_____

_____

_____

_____

3.

_____

_____

_____

_____

2.

_____

_____

_____

_____

4.

_____

_____

_____

_____

Name _____

Use the words in the box to fill in each blank. Write your own answer for the second part of number 4.

| equal | triangles | squares | rectangles | circles | three | four |

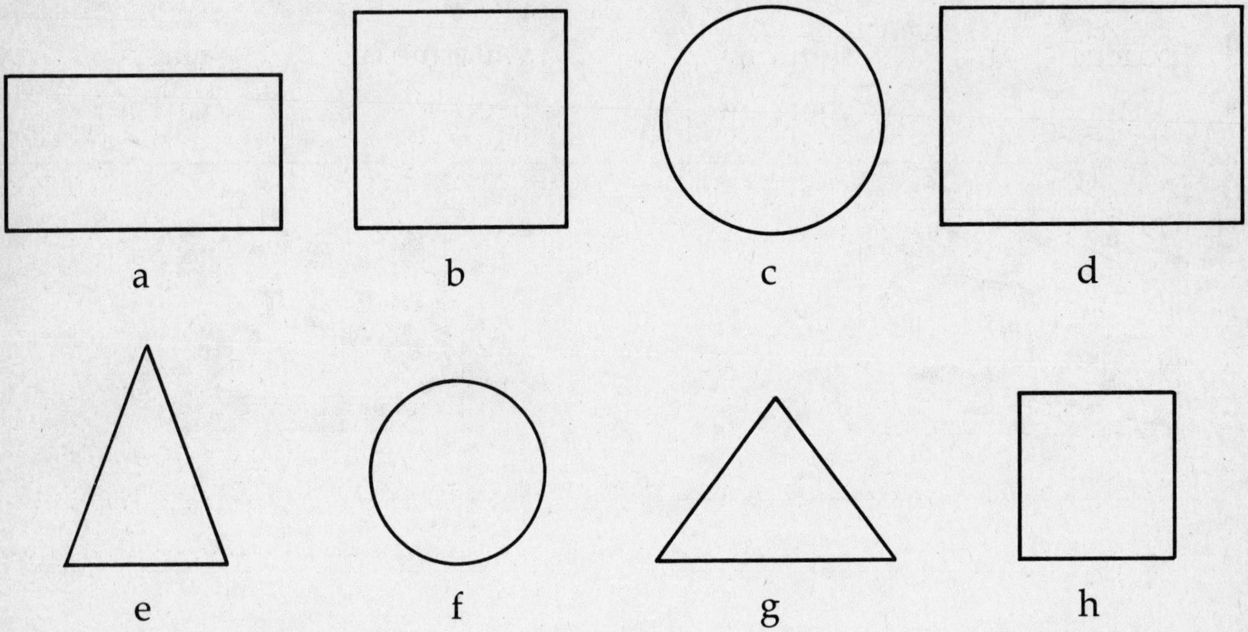

a

b

c

d

e

f

g

h

1. Figures **e** and **g** are _____.

   Each has _____ sides.

2. **A** and **d** are _____.

   They have _____ sides.

3. **B** and **h** are _____.

   They have four _____ sides.

4. **C** and **f** are _____.

   How many sides do they have? _____

   _____

Name

Critical Thinking, Level C © 1993 Steck-Vaughn

A **kitten** is a kind of **cat** which is a kind of **animal**.

Each sentence has two blanks. The first missing word will come from **list 1**. The second missing word will come from **list 2**.

List 1		List 2	
circus	plane	head	year
shoe	fruit	room	tree
sentences	door	food	clothing
branch	face	stories	transportation
room	month	building	entertainment

1. A **sandal** is a kind of _____ which is part of our _____ .

2. A **peach** is a kind of _____ which is a kind of _____ .

3. A **knob** is part of a _____ which is part of a _____ .

4. **Words** are parts of _____ which are parts of _____ .

5. A **leaf** is part of a _____ which is part of a _____ .

6. A **door** is part of a _____ which is part of a _____ .

7. A **wing** is part of a _____ which is a kind of _____ .

8. A **nose** is part of a _____ which is part of a _____ .

9. A **clown** is part of a _____ which is a kind of _____ .

10. **July** is a _____ which is part of a _____ .

Name

Read the article below. Then list the sound signals and sight signals on the lines below the headings.

Signals

Long ago, signals were often used to send messages from one person to another. The people who sent and received signals had to know what each signal meant. Signals were sent by making sounds or by using signs.

Some of the first signals were made by beating drums or by using a funnel as a loudspeaker. Fires, smoke signals, and lanterns were also used.

Some of the signals that are now used are bells, bugles, whistles, sirens, foghorns, flags, banners, blinking lights, beacon lights, and flares. Over long distances, messages are sent by radio in codes that use dots and dashes.

Sound   **Sight**

_____   _____

_____   _____

_____   _____

_____   _____

_____   _____

_____   _____

_____   _____

Name _____

A. Put **R** before each name of a real person. Put **F** before each name of a fanciful or make-believe being.

1. _____ genie   5. _____ troll   9. _____ electrician

2. _____ farmer   6. _____ teacher   10. _____ elf

3. _____ ghost   7. _____ plumber   11. _____ monster

4. _____ lawyer   8. _____ painter   12. _____ leprechaun

B. Fanciful beings may be used in a sentence about something that could really happen. Mark each sentence **R** for real or **F** for fanciful.

_____ 1. The child wrote a story about a ghost.

_____ 2. Della played with an elf after school.

_____ 3. There are many movies about monsters.

_____ 4. Children dressed up as leprechauns on Halloween.

_____ 5. A troll got into our pond and made a great deal of trouble.

_____ 6. The genie granted my wish for a new bicycle.

C.   1. Write your own sentence about something fanciful or make-believe.

_____

_____

2. Write a sentence that tells about something that could really happen.

_____

_____

Name _____

A. Here are two books about horses. Book **X** tells real things about horses. Book **Y** is a fairy tale. It tells about things that horses really could not be or do. Look at the sentences below. On the line, write the letter of the book in which you would expect to read the sentence.

1. _____ Horses like to eat hay.

2. _____ Horses are purple.

3. _____ Horses have four legs.

4. _____ Horses can talk.

5. _____ Horses wear socks.

6. _____ Horses are good pets.

7. _____ Horses can shop.

8. _____ Horses fix supper.

X

Y

B. 1. Write a sentence that tells something a horse can really do.

_____

_____

2. Write a fanciful sentence about a horse.

_____

_____

_____

Name _____

Critical Thinking, Level C © 1993 Steck-Vaughn

A **fact** can be proved to be true. An **opinion** tells only what someone thinks or believes.

Fact:
Two plus two equals four.

Opinion:
Four is a lucky number.

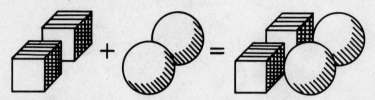 

Read each sentence below. Put **F** before each fact and **O** before each opinion.

_____ 1. Softball is the best game to play.

_____ 2. Leon came into class after the bell rang.

_____ 3. Winter is the most enjoyable season of the year.

_____ 4. Some horses live on the plains.

_____ 5. January is a good month to have a birthday.

_____ 6. A meter is smaller than a mile.

_____ 7. Sunday is the first day of the week.

_____ 8. The earth is over two hundred years old.

_____ 9. It is more important to be kind than to be honest.

_____ 10. Brazil is the most beautiful country in the world.

_____ 11. Alaska is the largest state in the United States.

_____ 12. Toronto is a great place to visit.

_____ 13. Dogs are better pets than cats.

_____ 14. Snakes and lizards are both reptiles.

Name _____

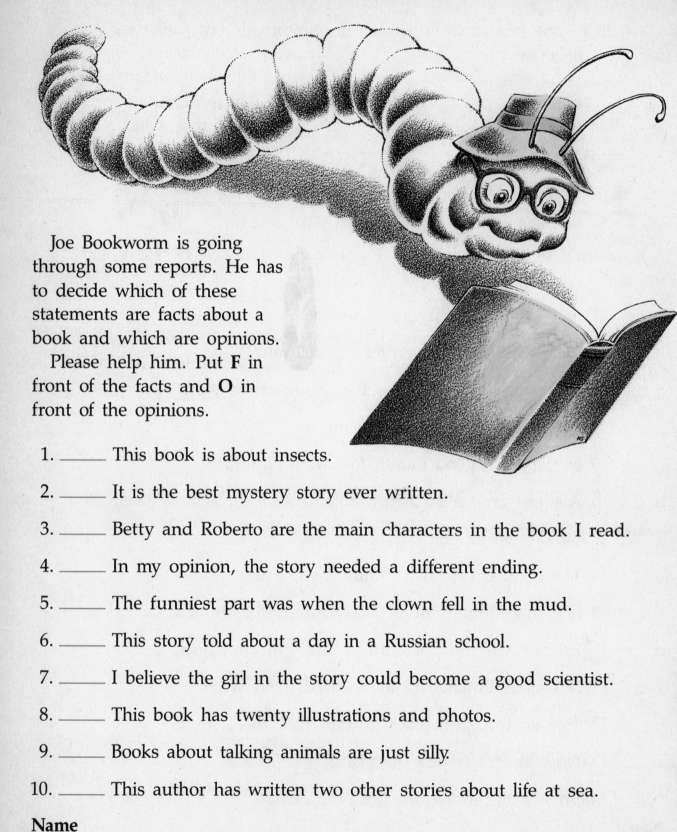

Joe Bookworm is going through some reports. He has to decide which of these statements are facts about a book and which are opinions.

Please help him. Put **F** in front of the facts and **O** in front of the opinions.

1. _____ This book is about insects.

2. _____ It is the best mystery story ever written.

3. _____ Betty and Roberto are the main characters in the book I read.

4. _____ In my opinion, the story needed a different ending.

5. _____ The funniest part was when the clown fell in the mud.

6. _____ This story told about a day in a Russian school.

7. _____ I believe the girl in the story could become a good scientist.

8. _____ This book has twenty illustrations and photos.

9. _____ Books about talking animals are just silly.

10. _____ This author has written two other stories about life at sea.

Name

Critical Thinking, Level C © 1993 Steck-Vaughn

Can you find the mistakes below? The first eight sentences should be facts, or things that we know are true. The next eight sentences should be opinions, or things that some people think are true. Put **X** before each sentence that is not under the right heading.

Facts

_____ 1. A plane can cross the ocean faster than a ship.

_____ 2. Ice will not last very long in a warm room.

_____ 3. Bowling is more fun than swimming.

_____ 4. Most people go to the circus to see the clowns.

_____ 5. The team chose Keith as the best player in today's game.

_____ 6. A tiger's babies are called cubs.

_____ 7. Mountain bikes are better than racing bikes.

_____ 8. Trees are used to make paper.

Opinions

_____ 1. A picnic is more fun than a meal at home.

_____ 2. Your mother's brother is your uncle.

_____ 3. You will enjoy a visit to Walt Disney World.

_____ 4. Nothing good happens on rainy days.

_____ 5. A feather is not as heavy as a rock of the same size.

_____ 6. Dirty hands are a sign of a messy person.

_____ 7. Summer vacations are nicer than winter ones.

_____ 8. Apples grow on trees, but grapes grow on vines.

Name _____

A. The picture shows a kite. Below are some statements of fact about the kite. Write two sentences of your own about the kite that state facts.

- The kite is diamond-shaped.

- The kite is made of paper and light wood.

- The kite has a design on it.

1. _____

_____

_____

2. _____

_____

B. These sentences state some opinions about the kite. Write two more sentences that tell your opinions about kites.

- The kite is a delightful toy.

- The kite is flying very gracefully.

- Diamond-shaped kites are better than box kites.

1. _____

_____

2. _____

_____

Name _____

When you give the meaning of a word, you give its **definition**. For example, a **mammal** is a warm-blooded animal that has hair, lungs, and a backbone.	When you name things that belong to a group, you give **examples**. For instance, **cows, dogs, mice**, and **apes** are mammals.

Each sentence gives either a definition or an example. If it gives a definition, put **D** after the sentence. If it gives an example, put **E** after the sentence.

1. A reptile is a cold-blooded animal that crawls or creeps. _____

2. Evergreen trees are trees such as pines, firs, and redwoods. _____

3. A kangaroo is a mammal that has small front legs and large

    hind legs. _____

4. Iron, gold, silver, and tin are metals. _____

5. Bats are mammals that hang upside down during the day. _____

6. An island is a piece of land surrounded by water. _____

7. Beavers are mammals that build dams. _____

8. Notions are things such as needles, pins, snaps, and buttons. _____

9. A container is an object used for holding or carrying things. _____

10. Some islands of the Pacific are Fiji, the Solomon Islands, and

    New Caledonia. _____

Name _____

A **definition** gives the meaning of a word. **Examples** of the same word are names of things which belong to its group. Read each definition below. Then look at the bottom of the page to find the word that fits the definition. Write the word on the line in the middle of the page. Next, find examples of this word. Write the letter of the examples on the line before the definition.

Definition		Example
____ 1. animals covered with feathers	_____	A. robins, owls, sparrows
____ 2. shelters with a roof, floor, and walls	_____	B. saw, hammer, pliers
____ 3. things to put on a bed	_____	C. moths, fleas, crickets
____ 4. tiny animals with six legs	_____	D. barn, house, garage
____ 5. things to help do work	_____	E. blankets, pillows, sheets

bedding	insects	buildings	tools	birds

Critical Thinking, Level C © 1993 Steck-Vaughn

Name

Find the definition of each word in a dictionary. Write the definition on the line after **definition**. Then write at least two examples on the line after **examples**.

1. holiday   definition: _____

   _____

   examples: _____

2. reptile   definition: _____

   _____

   examples: _____

3. cereal   definition: _____

   _____

   examples: _____

4. tree   definition: _____

   _____

   examples: _____

5. profession   definition: _____

   _____

   examples: _____

6. fowl   definition: _____

   _____

   examples: _____

Name _____

For each puzzle, a definition and examples are provided. Use the definition and examples to figure out the word. Write it in the puzzle. The first one is done for you.

heavenly body that orbits the sun

1. Large towns where people live and work

2. The blossom of a plant

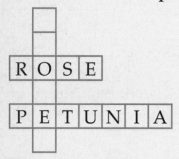

3. One of the twelve periods of time making up a year

4. Something played for fun

5. Tall plant with a trunk and leaves

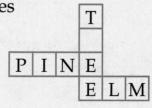

6. Sweet food served at the end of a meal

P U D D I N G

B R O W N I E S

Name _____

A **summary** sums up or tells briefly what a paragraph or story is about. A summary tells the main facts or ideas. It does not give all the details.

Read the paragraph below. Then use the word box to complete the summary that follows.

> Sea life is often divided into three groups: plankton, animals that swim, and plants and animals that live on the sea's floor. Plankton include tiny plants and animals that drift through the sea in large groups. Plant plankton are important because they make oxygen, a gas needed by all animals. The animals that swim include fish, whales, turtles, and octopuses. These swimming animals are mostly hunters. They eat other fish for food. Usually, big fish eat little fish. However, huge whales eat tiny plankton. Many plants and animals live only at the bottom of the sea. In this group are crabs, lobsters, snails, coral, and sponges. Many of these animals eat plankton, and many are food themselves for the swimmers of the sea.

crabs	floor	sea	smaller
plankton	animal	float	sponges

Life in the _____ includes _____, swimmers,

and plants and animals that live on the ocean _____.
Plankton are tiny plants and animals that do not swim but

_____. The swimmers include any sea _____ that

swims, and the bottom dwellers include _____,

_____, and coral. Most sea animals feed on _____

fish or plants.

Name _____

A. Read the paragraph and the three summaries that follow it. Then copy the summary that best explains the main idea of the paragraph.

The words that we use in the English language keep changing. Some words are dropped because they describe things no longer used. For instance, a **shongable** was a tax on shoes that people had to pay in the 1400s. Now the tax is gone and so is the word. Other words go out of style because they are hard to say. **Mubblefubbles**, which means sadness, is one example.

1. Words change because they are hard to pronounce.

2. Words in a language change for many reasons.

3. Words are dropped because they name out-of-date things.

_____

_____

B. Read the paragraph below. Then complete the summary.

The first airplane flight across the United States was made in 1911. It was a very difficult flight! The plane had no radio, and there was no parachute for the pilot. These things had not yet been invented. The trip took about 46 days, but only three of those were in the air! The rest of the time the plane was on the ground for repairs. The fact that there were no airports then did not help.

The first cross-country _____ took 46 _____

and faced many _____.

Name _____

Critical Thinking, Level C © 1993 Steck-Vaughn

Read each paragraph below. Find the words that tell what the paragraph is about. We call these words the **main idea**. Write the main idea on the line below the title. The first word has been written for you. Now write the facts from the paragraph on the lines below the main idea.

There are many names for homes. A palace is a large home for a ruler to live in. A mansion is smaller than a palace. A house is where a family often lives. A cottage is a very small house of wood or stone.

Homes

★ Many _____

A. _____

B. _____

C. _____

D. _____

Seeds travel in many ways. Birds drop them. Winds carry them. Insects bring seeds on their feet. Seeds stick to animals' fur and are moved along. Some seeds fall to the ground from bushes and trees.

Seeds

★ _____

A. _____

B. _____

C. _____

D. _____

E. _____

Name _____

23

Read each statement. Decide what the main idea of that statement is. Write the main idea on the line in the outline that has **main idea** printed after it. Then write the facts below the main idea. When you are through, see if you can write a longer story using the same outline.

I. A home aquarium should have a filter, a heater, and a thermometer.
II. The things you can put in it are plants, snails, tropical fish, and gravel.
III. Tanks need care. You must wash them out and see that they do not leak.

Tank

I. _____ **(main idea)**

   A. _____ (fact)

   B. _____ (fact)

   C. _____ (fact)

II. _____ **(main idea)**

   A. _____ (fact)

   B. _____ (fact)

   C. _____ (fact)

   D. _____ (fact)

III. _____ **(main idea)**

   A. _____ (fact)

   B. _____ (fact)

Name _____

Critical Thinking, Level C © 1993 Steck-Vaughn

A. — **Real and Fanciful**

Read each pair of sentences. Write R if the sentence tells about something that could happen. Write F if it tells about something fanciful.

1. _____ The tiny <u>elves</u> quickly made boots.

    _____ That <u>shoemaker</u> carefully fixed my old shoes.

2. _____ An <u>eagle</u> soared high into the sky.

    _____ The <u>unicorn</u> flew into the clouds.

3. _____ A <u>leprechaun</u> buried the pot of gold.

    _____ The <u>miner</u> worked underground searching for diamonds.

B. — **Classifying**
Outlining and Summarizing

Read the underlined words in the sentences above. Decide whether each word names something real or something fanciful. Write each word under the correct main idea in the outline below.

I. Fanciful

    A. _____

    B. _____

    C. _____

II. Real

    A. _____

    B. _____

    C. _____

Name _____

25

C. Definition and Example

The picture shows three floors of a store. The definitions on the left tell what kind of thing you can find on each floor. Under each definition, write the correct word from the box. Then study the sign to find examples of each definition. Write the examples on the lines at the right to show on which floor you would find them.

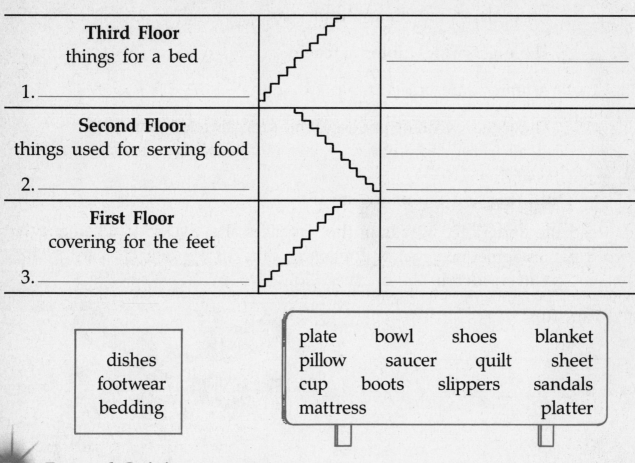

Third Floor
things for a bed

1. _____

Second Floor
things used for serving food

2. _____

First Floor
covering for the feet

3. _____

dishes
footwear
bedding

plate   bowl   shoes   blanket
pillow   saucer   quilt   sheet
cup   boots   slippers   sandals
mattress   platter

D. Fact and Opinion

Complete the two parts of the sentence to make it tell your opinion.

The best floor in the store is the _____ because _____

_____ .

Name

Critical Thinking, Level C © 1993 Steck-Vaughn

Understanding

Understanding means telling about something in your own words. Let's try it out. What can you say about the boy in the picture? How does he feel? How do you know? Do you think he would rather be someplace else? Have you ever felt the way he probably feels?

1. Circle the things that are found on a playground.

   diving board   swings   seesaw   slide

2. Circle the things that are alive.

   babies   flowers   rocks   sand

3. Circle the things that are hard to break.

   iron   butter   bricks   crackers   concrete

4. Circle the animals that live on land.

   goats   fish   horses   camels   whales

5. Circle the things that you might fill with air.

   balloon   wall   football   tire   pool

6. Circle the things that you can drink.

   milk   crackers   water   juice   bread

7. Circle the things that are heavy to lift.

   elephant   truck   kite   stove   TV

8. Circle the things that can make a loud noise.

   firecracker   sponge   horn   drum   mop

Name

Critical Thinking, Level C © 1993 Steck-Vaughn

1	2	3	4	5	6

alarm	Arabic	hands	round
watch	face	Roman	

A. Complete the sentences using the words in the box.

1. All of the clocks have a _____ and two _____.

2. The faces are all _____.

3. Some of the clocks have _____ numerals. Some have

   _____ numerals.

4. Picture **4** is an _____ clock.

5. Picture **1** is a _____.

B. Answer the sentences using the numbers under each clock.

1. Which is the most decorated clock? _____

2. Which clock has a glass case all around it? _____

3. Which one do you think is called a banjo clock? _____

4. Which one has weights hanging from it? _____

Name

A. Read each sentence. Then underline the statement that tells how the three things are alike.

1. How are dolphins, parrots, and dogs alike?
   a. They are all house pets.
   b. They are all animals.
   c. They all have feet.

2. How are staples, paper clips, and rubber bands alike?
   a. They are all made of shiny metal.
   b. They can all be stretched to different sizes.
   c. They are all used to hold things together.

3. How are books, magazines, and newspapers alike?
   a. They all have hard covers.
   b. They all have printed words in them.
   c. They are all sold at newsstands.

4. How are plums, peaches, and cherries alike?
   a. They all have fuzzy skins.
   b. They all have pits.
   c. They are all the same size.

B. Write a sentence that tells how the items in each group are alike.

1. knife, fork, spoon

_____

2. curtains, shades, shutters

_____

Name _____

Critical Thinking, Level C © 1993 Steck-Vaughn

All letters have the same kind of plan. This plan shows the parts of a letter. Use the plan to fill in the blanks in the paragraph about letters.

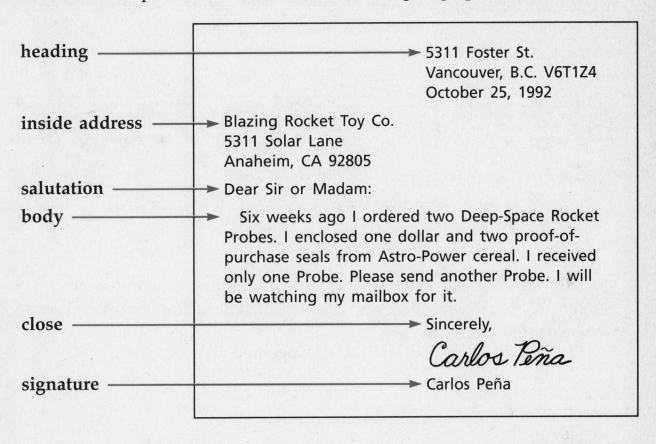

heading ———————————→ 5311 Foster St.
Vancouver, B.C. V6T1Z4
October 25, 1992

inside address ————→ Blazing Rocket Toy Co.
5311 Solar Lane
Anaheim, CA 92805

salutation ——————→ Dear Sir or Madam:

body —————————→   Six weeks ago I ordered two Deep-Space Rocket Probes. I enclosed one dollar and two proof-of-purchase seals from Astro-Power cereal. I received only one Probe. Please send another Probe. I will be watching my mailbox for it.

close —————————→ Sincerely,

                                 Carlos Peña

signature ————————→ Carlos Peña

Letters have parts that appear in order. They begin with the writer's address and date, which is called the _____. They end with the writer's _____ . The _____, which appears after the heading, gives the name of the person receiving the letter. The _____ greets the person or company to whom the letter is addressed. The writer's message is contained in the _____ . The brief good-bye following the body is called the _____ .

Name _____

A. Stories, pictures, music, and many other things follow a plan. Look at the plan for these two lines of music. They are the same except for two notes in each line. Circle the notes where the plan of the music is different.

B. Most stories have the same kind of plan. Of course, the words are different. This drawing shows a story's plan. Fill in the blanks in the story with the words that fit.

6. exciting point

7. problem is solved

1. beginning
2. characters
3. time
4. place

5. things happen

8. ends

A story has a _____. This often tells you who the _____ are. It usually gives the _____ and the _____. Then _____. The story reaches an _____. Finally, the _____, and the story _____.

Name _____

A. Put the following steps in order. Write **1** on the line before the first step in each group. Number the rest until the last step has a **4** before it.

1. Washing Dishes

_____ Wash the dishes.

_____ Dry the dishes.

_____ Fill the sink with water.

_____ Put away the dishes.

2. Getting Ready for School

_____ Leave home.

_____ Eat and get dressed.

_____ Board the school bus.

_____ Get up.

3. Making a Model Airplane

_____ Display the finished model.

_____ Gather the materials.

_____ Paint the assembled model.

_____ Put together the model.

4. Baking a Cake

_____ Mix the ingredients.

_____ Bake the cake.

_____ Gather the ingredients.

_____ Frost the cake.

B. What steps do you follow when you make a peanut butter and jelly sandwich? Write the steps below. Number the steps beginning with **1**.

_____

_____

_____

_____

_____

_____

Name _____

A. Read the directions for wrapping a present. Then number the sentences from **1** to **5** to show the correct order of the steps.

Wrapping a Present

To wrap a present you must first gather the materials. You will need a gift, a box to hold the gift, wrapping paper, tape, and ribbon. Place the gift in the box. Spread out the wrapping paper and, in the center, place the box containing the gift. Neatly fold the wrapping paper around the box and smooth out all wrinkles. Then tape the paper into place. Finally, tie a ribbon around the box and add a bow.

_____ Put the gift into the box.

_____ Fold the paper around the box.

_____ Tape the paper.

_____ Put a ribbon and a bow on the wrapped box.

_____ Gather the necessary materials.

B. Read the paragraph. Then number the pictures from **1** to **4** to show the correct order of the steps in a frog's life.

A Frog's Life

A frog begins its life as a small egg in water. A tadpole, which looks like a little fish, emerges when the egg hatches. The tadpole changes as it grows. It develops legs and lungs, and it loses its gills. Finally, a little frog with a tiny tail emerges from the water to live on land.

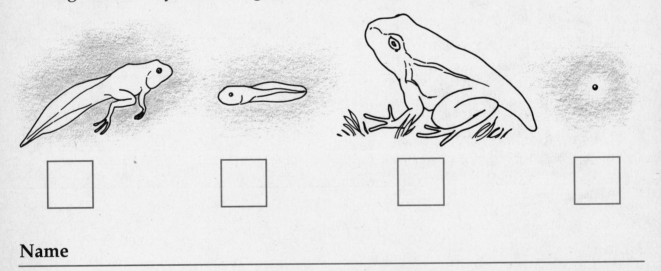

Name _____

Write the word (or words) in the blank that completes each sentence. Use the map to find your answers.

1. Route 20 crosses _____.
        Mad River   Fox River   no river

2. The school is _____.
        near the library   on Route 20   near the subdivision

3. People shop on _____.
        Center Street   Mountain Road   Valley Road

4. The subdivision is closest to _____.
        the library   the stores   Valley Road

5. Main Street runs _____.
        north and south   east and west

Name

Figural Relationships

You can find many squares, rectangles, and triangles in the figure below. Some of the shapes are not easy to find. First, find all the squares and write the number on the line below. Next, find all the rectangles. Finally, find the triangles. You might use three different colors of crayons to trace the three different kinds of shapes.

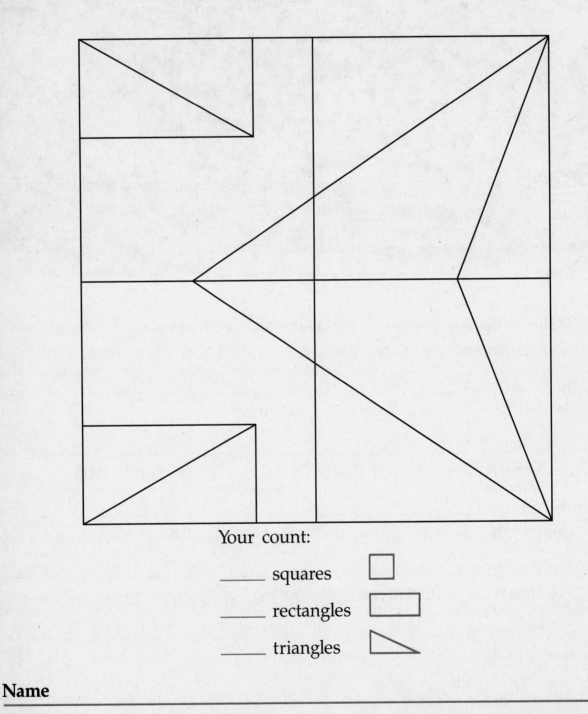

Your count:

_____ squares

_____ rectangles

_____ triangles

Name

Critical Thinking, Level C © 1993 Steck-Vaughn

Comparing Word Meanings

A. Write a word from the box below that means the same as each word shown.

> tired   build   help   afraid   under

1. scared   ___ ___ ☐ ___ ___ ___

2. construct   ___ ☐ ___ ___ ___

3. assist   ___ ___ ☐ ___

4. beneath   ___ ___ ___ ___ ☐ ___

5. exhausted   ___ ___ ☐ ___ ___

Write the letters from the boxes in order to finish the answer to this riddle.

Riddle: When is a piece of wood like a king?

Answer: When it's a ☐ ☐ ☐ ☐ ☐

B. Write a word from the box below that is the opposite of each word shown.

> wrong   seldom   small   arrive

1. leave   ☐ ___ ___ ___ ___

2. often   ☐ ___ ___ ___ ___ ___

3. enormous   ___ ___ ☐ ___ ___

4. right   ☐ ___ ___ ___ ___

Write the letters from the boxes in order to answer this riddle.

Riddle: What has a thousand teeth but no mouth?

Answer: ☐ ☐ ☐ ☐

Name

Read the story. Then follow the directions to complete parts **A** and **B**.

A Fanciful Tale

The hike was almost over. Tom, Tim, and Tina were looking forward to leaving the woods. Their legs were weary. Their backpacks seemed heavy. "Oh," Tom exclaimed, "I'll be glad to take off this backpack!"
"Good," buzzed a mosquito. "Let's see what you have left to eat."
"Nothing for you," said Tom crossly. He slapped at the pesky mosquito.
"You're rude," said the mosquito, dodging Tom's hand. And it bit Tom on the nose.

A. Use a word from the story to complete these sentences.

　　1. Another word for **tired** is _____.

　　2. The insect named in the story is a _____.

　　3. When Tom spoke **angrily**, he spoke _____.

　　4. Tom was told he was impolite, or _____.

　　5. The bug avoided Tom's hand by _____ it.

B. Use a word from the box to complete these sentences.

entertaining	annoying	imaginary	hit	weighty

　　1. **Fanciful** means _____.

　　2. Another word for **heavy** is _____.

　　3. When Tom slapped at the bug, he tried to _____ it.

　　4. The insect was _____ Tom.

　　5. A story like this is _____, but not true.

Name _____

Read each paragraph. Copy the items in the box to fill in the main idea and details of the paragraph.

1. Honeybees are insects that produce honey, a food eaten by humans. The wax from their honeycombs is used to make useful things such as candles. Bees fertilize plants as they fly from flower to flower. Honeybees are very helpful to people.

Bees make honey.	Bees fertilize flowers.
Beeswax is used to make useful things.	Honeybees help people.

Main Idea: _____

Details: a. _____

          b. _____

          c. _____

2. Despite the cold, there is much to do outside in the winter. Some people ice-skate on frozen ponds. Others go sledding down snow-covered hills. Many go cross-country and downhill skiing.

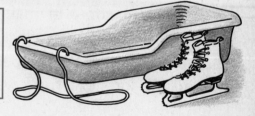

go skiing	ice-skate on ponds
things to do outside in winter	sled down hills

Main Idea: _____

Details: a. _____

          b. _____

          c. _____

Name _____

39

The **main idea** tells what a story is about. Circle one sentence in each story that gives the main idea. Draw a line through any sentence that does not belong in a story.

1. Ants build many kinds of nests. Some dig tunnels in the earth and pile dirt above the ground. Termites also burrow. Some ants live in hollow trees. Other ants use sticky leaves to build nests.

2. Babies cry to tell us something. They cry when they are hungry. They cry when they are hurt or afraid. They cry when they have wet diapers. It is fun to play with dolls.

3. Most birds build their nests in the branches of trees. Other animals live in trees, too. Some birds build their nests along the gutters of buildings. Birds have even been known to build nests on jungle gyms in playgrounds. You never know where you'll find a bird nest!

4. Watches come in many different styles. Some watches are digital, while others have regular clock faces. Many watches tell the date as well as the time. Today is September 2. There are sport watches, dressy watches, and all sorts of "fun" watches.

5. Checkers is a good indoor game, and hopscotch is a good outdoor game. As you can tell, games can be played both indoors and out. Most board games are played indoors. So are card games. Outdoor games include those that use balls and involve running. Bicycling is fun outdoors, too.

Name

Critical Thinking, Level C © 1993 Steck-Vaughn

For each story on this page, write **main idea** on the line after the words that tell what the story is about. Write **fact** on the line after the words which add something to the meaning of the story. Put **X** on the line after the words that tell a fact that is not in the story.

1.   There are about 240 kinds of turtles in the world. They vary greatly in size. Some can put their legs and head entirely inside their shells, but others cannot.

beautiful   put heads inside their   many kinds of

shells _____   shells _____   turtles _____

2.   The light bulb was only one of many inventions by Thomas A. Edison. He worked on it for many years. The invention was completed in 1879. It changed the way people lived and worked.

the electric light   invention completed   many uses for

bulb _____   in 1879 _____   electricity _____

3.   A beehive houses worker bees, nurse bees, male bees called drones, and one queen. The hive is made up of cells that form a comb. In the spring and summer the workers fill the cells with honey.

one kind of bee,   the buzzing of bees   what a beehive

the worker _____ _____   contains _____

4.   Some bicycle races are held on sloping tracks that are oval in shape. One such race is called a Madison. In a Madison, cyclists race in teams of two. The teammates take turns racing and resting until they have completed the required number of laps.

how to fix a   what a Madison   an oval sloping

bicycle _____   is like _____   track _____

Name _____

Read each story. Copy the title below it that best states the main idea.

1. One of the most common kinds of boats on a river is the barge. It is a long, low boat with a flat bottom. Barges are used to carry heavy things such as logs, sand, and cement. Most barges do not have their own engines. Instead, they are pushed by strong tugboats.

River Traffic   Learning About Barges   How Tugboats Work

2. No harbor is complete without buoys. Buoys are floating objects that help sailors and boaters steer safely through the tricky waters near shore. Some buoys show that the water is too shallow for boats. Others warn of rocks or mark the path a boat should follow. Buoys may have bells, whistles, or flashing lights.

Bells and Whistles   Harbor Helpers   Floating Objects

3. A houseboat is built more for living than for sailing. Most houseboats are tied up at docks in calm waters. Although some people in North America live on houseboats, they are in much greater use in Asia. In places such as Hong Kong, where land is scarce, thousands of people live on houseboats.

Houseboats in Asia   Sailing on Houseboats   Facts About Houseboats

Name

A. This lesson is just for fun. Use the letters of the alphabet in place of words.

A   B   C   D   E   F

1. an insect   B

2. another word for ocean   _____

G   H   I   J   K   L

3. girl's name   _____

4. a part of your face   _____

5. a blue bird   _____

M   N   O   P   Q   R

6. a word that shows surprise   _____

7. a vegetable   _____

S   T   U   V   W   X   Y   Z

8. a kind of drink   _____

9. yourself   _____

10. a word that asks a question   _____

B. In the sentences below, use letters in place of the words.

1. Oh, I see you.   _____

2. Be seein' you.   _____

3. Are you okay?   _____

Name

> **Rules:**
> 1. Share with other people.
> 2. Do not rush into the street without looking.
> 3. Wash your hands before you eat.
> 4. Do not play with matches.
> 5. Obey your parents.

At the top of the page are some rules. Some short stories are below. Write the number of the rule before the story it matches.

_____ Lupe got two sets of paints for her birthday. She really needed only one, so she asked Mark if he would like to use one too.

_____ Lee watched his baby brother playing on the floor. Suddenly, Lee jumped up and quickly picked something off the floor. He put the book of matches safely away in a drawer.

_____ Jeff sometimes forgot the good health rules his mother had taught him. Although she often tired of reminding him, she did not give up. One night Jeff found a washcloth instead of a napkin at his place at the dinner table.

_____ Wendy asked Jill to stop at the card store with her after school one day. Although Jill wanted to buy a card too, she remembered that her parents had told her to come right home from school and not stop anywhere else.

_____ Spring seemed a long time coming. Sue was eager to play baseball after school. The first really warm day, she dashed out of school and raced across the street.

Critical Thinking, Level C © 1993 Steck-Vaughn

Name _____

A. Choose the word that best fits each sentence. Write the word on the correct line.

rang	pencil	foggy	after
park	before	work	reward

1. If you are going to write, you will need a _____ .

2. I got my _____ because I did what my teacher asked.

3. If the sun shines, we are going on a trip to the _____ .

4. The bell _____ just as I finished.

5. Because the day is _____ , it is hard to see.

6. Since Nora ran faster, Bill finished _____ Nora.

7. You may go if you get your _____ finished.

8. April comes _____ May each year.

B. Use your own words to complete each sentence.

1. When it rains, you _____

_____

2. If you make a mistake, you _____

_____

Name _____

45

Think of questions you might ask to get each of the following answers. Write one question on the line above the answer. The first one is done for you.

1. Q: <u>Where did she hit the ball?</u>
   A: over the fence

2. Q: _____
   A: in the morning

3. Q: _____
   A: when it rains

4. Q: _____
   A: at the circus

5. Q: _____
   A: last Saturday

6. Q: _____
   A: a dark brown

7. Q: _____
   A: My brother did it.

8. Q: _____
   A: a barking dog

9. Q: _____
   A: in the lake

10. Q: _____
   A: beside the garage

Name _____

Critical Thinking, Level C © 1993 Steck-Vaughn

A. Identifying Main Ideas
Comparing Word Meanings
Identifying Figural Relationships

Read the paragraph and study the map. Use the information in the paragraph and the map to answer the questions.

Washington, D.C., has many places to visit. The White House is the home of the President of the United States. It is toured by over a million people every year. The Capitol is where Congress meets. The towering Washington Monument offers visitors a spectacular view from its top.

1. What is the main idea of the paragraph?

_____

2. Which place to visit is farther from the Washington Monument?

_____

3. Which word in the paragraph is another word for *outstanding?*

_____

B. Identifying Relationships

Circle the words a visitor could use to tell about a trip to the city of Washington, D.C.

tracks   beautiful   interesting   historic   shoe

Name _____

C. Comparing and Contrasting
Identifying Structure

Study the snowmen carefully. Find the **one** snowman that is missing what all the others have. Write down that snowman's letter next to 1. Next, find **two** snowmen that are missing what the others have. Write down those letters next to 2. Last, find **three** snowmen that are missing what the other snowman has. (You will write some letters more than once.)

1. _____ 2. _____ 3. _____

A   B   C   D

D. Identifying Steps in a Process

Choose one of the snowmen above. Write 5 steps to follow to make that snowman.

1. _____

2. _____

3. _____

4. _____

5. _____

Name _____

Critical Thinking, Level C © 1993 Steck-Vaughn

Applying

Applying means using what you know. Look at the picture. How does the girl feel? Why are her arms raised? Do you think it is a special day? What do you think she did to win the medal? Have you ever felt the way she appears to feel? Why?

Put each list of things in order. Write **1, 2, 3,** and **4** to show the correct order.

I. Put the things in list A in order from short to long. Do the same for list B.

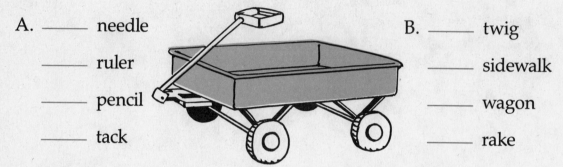

A. —— needle   B. —— twig

   —— ruler   —— sidewalk

   —— pencil   —— wagon

   —— tack   —— rake

II. Put the things in list C in order from small to large. Do the same for list D.

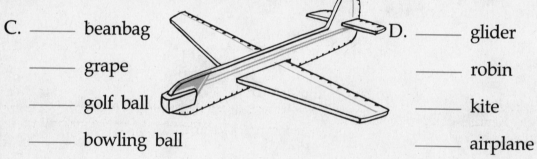

C. —— beanbag   D. —— glider

   —— grape   —— robin

   —— golf ball   —— kite

   —— bowling ball   —— airplane

III. Put the things in list E in order from easy work to hard work. Do the same for list F.

E. —— doing math   F. —— washing dishes

   —— writing words   —— making beds

   —— reading   —— sweeping floors

   —— singing   —— emptying trash

Name _____

Critical Thinking, Level C © 1993 Steck-Vaughn

Land animals move at different speeds. The cheetah is the fastest animal on land. Read each set of facts below. Put **1** on the line beside the fact in each set about the fastest animal. Number the rest until the slowest animal is labeled **4**.

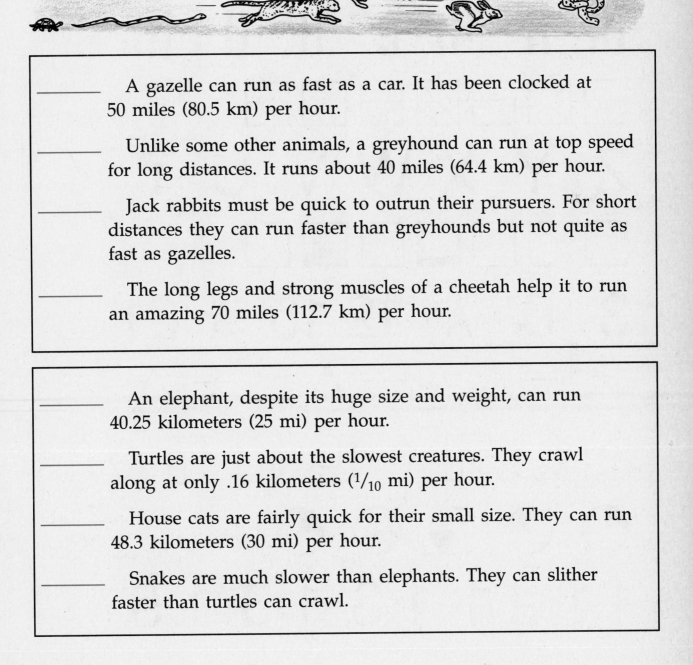

_____   A gazelle can run as fast as a car. It has been clocked at 50 miles (80.5 km) per hour.

_____   Unlike some other animals, a greyhound can run at top speed for long distances. It runs about 40 miles (64.4 km) per hour.

_____   Jack rabbits must be quick to outrun their pursuers. For short distances they can run faster than greyhounds but not quite as fast as gazelles.

_____   The long legs and strong muscles of a cheetah help it to run an amazing 70 miles (112.7 km) per hour.

_____   An elephant, despite its huge size and weight, can run 40.25 kilometers (25 mi) per hour.

_____   Turtles are just about the slowest creatures. They crawl along at only .16 kilometers ($^1/_{10}$ mi) per hour.

_____   House cats are fairly quick for their small size. They can run 48.3 kilometers (30 mi) per hour.

_____   Snakes are much slower than elephants. They can slither faster than turtles can crawl.

Name _____

Study the figures in each group. Find the pattern, and then draw or write the figure that should come next in the pattern.

1.

2. ||| || ||| ⋮ ||| || |||

3. (figures)

4. **Z Y X W V U T**

5. (squares)

6. **3   6   ★   12   15   ★   21**

7. (figures)

8. (figures)

9. (circles with shaded sections)

10. 1×1 $1 + 1$ 1×3 $1 + 3$ 1×5

Name

Critical Thinking, Level C © 1993 Steck-Vaughn

A. Put a check before the activity in each pair that you could probably do faster.

1. _____ brush your teeth　　　　2. _____ paint the house

   _____ sharpen a pencil　　　　　　_____ wash the windows

3. _____ play a game of checkers　4. _____ go swimming

   _____ take out the trash　　　　　_____ take a trip to Canada

5. _____ feed the dog　　　　　　6. _____ clean your room

   _____ rake leaves in the yard　　　_____ eat a cookie

B. Which of the three answers below each question is closest to being correct? Put a check before the answer you choose.

1. It takes you two minutes to run around the block. How many minutes will it take you to walk around the block?

   _____ twenty　　　　_____ two　　　　_____ ten

2. How long does it take you to tie your shoe?

   _____ one hour　　　_____ ten minutes　　　_____ half a minute

3. How long does it take you to take a bath?

   _____ four seconds　　_____ fifteen minutes　　_____ two hours

4. You can put ten cookies into this box.　　How many can you put into this box?

   _____ two　　　_____ twelve　　　_____ twenty

Name _____

This map shows a castle or fort from the Middle Ages. A ditch filled with water, called a **moat**, could be crossed by lowering the drawbridge. The family lived in the tall tower, called a **keep**.

Use the scale beside the picture to see how far thirty meters is on the map. Then estimate, or guess, the distance for each sentence below. Write your estimates on the lines.

1. The height of each tower by the drawbridge is _____ meters.

2. The length of the drawbridge is _____ meters.

3. The height of the keep is _____ meters.

4. The length of the stable building is _____ meters.

5. The distance from the main gate to the keep is _____ meters.

Name _____

Critical Thinking, Level C © 1993 Steck-Vaughn

Circle the word that tells how the person in each story probably feels.

1. The puppy tore open the new pillows. Beth was

   angry   happy   excited

2. Rosa needed to spell one more word correctly to win the spelling contest. She did not know the word. Rosa was

   delighted   upset   pleased

3. John was worried because he had missed so much school. His mother watched as he opened his report card. He had gotten very good grades. His mother felt

   troubled   proud   ashamed

4. Jose was in the school play. He did not know his part very well. It was time for him to go on stage. Jose was

   angry   glad   frightened

5. Nancy had hoped to go to camp. When the day came for her to leave home, Nancy was sick with the flu. Nancy was

   surprised   thrilled   sad

6. Jay entered his turtle in a race. Near the end of the race, his turtle moved ahead of the rest. Jay was

   pleased   bored   disappointed

7. Laura was in a rush getting ready for school. When she got there and found she had on two different colored socks, she was

   excited   embarrassed   tired

8. Chan did not expect a party on his birthday. When he got home from school and found several of his friends there, he was

   scared   angry   surprised

Name

Read each story. Put **X** before the words which tell what will probably happen.

1. David found some money in front of a man's house. He took the money to the man who lived there. The man gave him a reward of fifty cents. What will David probably do next?

_____ give the money away   _____ thank the man

_____ put the money in a bank   _____ find more money

2. Carla planted bean seeds in the garden. Since the plants came up, she has watered them each day. When the plants grow bigger, Carla will

_____ plant new seeds.   _____ pull up the plants.

_____ pick the beans.   _____ cut the leaves off.

3. The Tweeds went to the park for a picnic. They did not notice that they had sat near an anthill. The Tweeds ended up sharing their lunch with hundreds of ants. When the Tweeds picnic again, they will

_____ sit next to an anthill.   _____ avoid any anthills.

_____ bring an anteater.   _____ go to a different park.

4. Martha read a book she really liked. She was sorry when the story came to an end. When Martha goes to the library, she will probably

_____ take out the same book.   _____ find another book by the same author.

_____ find another book on the same subject.   _____ reread the book.

Name _____

A. If things usually happen a certain way, we say they will **probably** happen that way. If, for instance, the river in this picture usually floods in the spring, we could say that it will probably flood next spring, too. Decide whether each of the events below usually happens. Then put **X** before those that are probably true.

_____ 1. It will rain tomorrow.

_____ 2. If it rains, the sidewalks will be wet.

_____ 3. The stores will be more crowded in December than in January.

_____ 4. Our school will serve lunch, as it always has done.

_____ 5. We will have the same teacher ten years from now.

_____ 6. More people will take vacations in August than in October.

_____ 7. It will rain sometime in the next month or so.

B. In the space below, rewrite the sentences you did not mark. Change them so they will probably be true.

_____

_____

_____

_____

Name _____

Write your own sentences to answer these questions.

1. If all diseases were wiped off the face of Earth, how do you think life here would change?

_____

_____

2. If people stopped reading books, what do you think would happen?

_____

_____

3. What if the weather never changed? How would our lives change?

_____

_____

4. If Europe went to a common currency, what are some things that would change?

_____

_____

5. What if people could wear wings that would allow them to fly from place to place? How would our lives change?

_____

_____

_____

Name

Critical Thinking, Level C © 1993 Steck-Vaughn

Circle the letter of the best answer for each activity below.

1. The girl looked happy as she crossed home plate.
   a. She was the best player on the team.
   b. She scored the winning run.
   c. She liked baseball.

2. The astronaut wore a heavy space suit.
   a. The suit made it easier to walk on the moon.
   b. The suit was comfortable to wear on Earth.
   c. The astronaut could run easily in the suit on Earth.

3. They dressed themselves. Then they fixed something to eat.
   a. They fixed lunch.
   b. They fixed dinner.
   c. They fixed breakfast.

4. Fred did not want to be alone after he read the book.
   a. He read a funny story.
   b. He read a very sad story.
   c. He read a mystery.

5. Jane ran faster and faster. She broke the tape.
   a. She won the race.
   b. She finished last.
   c. She was not supposed to break the tape.

Name _____

A. Which sentences do you think go together? Draw a line to show the ones that belong together. The first one is done for you.

1. The children are playing in the snow.

2. Chiang is opening presents.

3. Billy is afraid to ride his bicycle.

4. We are moving to another town.

5. He is a poor sport.

a. Last week he fell off and got hurt.

b. It is cold outside.

c. Children don't enjoy playing with him.

d. It is his birthday.

e. We will be living in a different house.

B. Read each sentence in color. Copy the sentence in black that best goes with it.

1. Selma plays kickball very well.

a. Children often choose her for their teams.
b. Tennis is her favorite sport.

_____

2. Sam has a pony.

a. He is afraid of horses.
b. He likes to ride.

_____

3. Lucio is ill today.

a. He was ill last week.
b. He won't go to school.

_____

4. Dale hasn't finished her homework.

a. She won't get to watch TV tonight.
b. She is an honors student.

_____

Name

Critical Thinking, Level C © 1993 Steck-Vaughn

Each of these sentences tells about something that happened. Below the sentences are reasons for the things that happened. Write the correct reason on the line below each sentence to explain what happened.

1. When Sally came home from school, she saw that the snow was gone.

    _____

2. In the afternoon, the students crossed the street with the crossing guard.

    _____

3. Something was bumping against the ceiling.

    _____

4. A puddle of water was under the open window and the curtains were wet.

    _____

5. The students and teachers left the school in a hurry and stood outside quietly.

    _____

Reasons

A. They were having a party.

B. It had been raining very hard.

C. The fire bell had rung.

D. School was over for the day.

E. A bird flew through the open window.

F. The sun had warmed the air.

G. The train was late.

Name

Read each story. Then write the best answer from the word box for the story.

1. John was sitting with his classmates in the front row. They were listening to the principal. She was calling out the names of students who had won awards during the year. John was in the

playground	auditorium	office

_____.

2. Sue and Percy were watching their favorite team on television. The score was tied in the bottom of the ninth inning. Then the team's best hitter came to bat. Sue and Percy were watching

football	basketball	baseball

_____.

3. Mei was looking forward to visiting her grandmother. They were going to see the baby chicks and ducklings, and then go for a ride on the new tractor. Mei's grandmother lived

in an apartment	on a farm	at the beach

_____.

4. From his house, Rudy can see rocky cliffs and snow-capped peaks. He likes to look down at the valley far below him. Rudy lives

on an island	in a city	in the mountains

_____.

5. Mrs. Reed listened to the radio before she went to work. On this day she wore a jacket but put her umbrella in her briefcase. The weather forecast on the radio called for

rain	snow	sunny skies

_____.

Name

Critical Thinking, Level C © 1993 Steck-Vaughn

A. Sometimes a word has two or more meanings. Study the words and their pictured meanings. Read each sentence below. Think about the underlined word. Write A or B to show which meaning the word has.

1. _____ She filled the pitcher with lemonade.

2. _____ The pitcher threw the ball to first base.

3. _____ The spaceship will launch in thirty minutes.

4. _____ The tiny launch pulled up to the dock.

B. Each underlined word has several meanings. Read each sentence. Then write a sentence in which the word has a different meaning.

1. The woodpecker clung to the bark of the tree.

_____

2. The chef poured the cake batter into the pan.

_____

3. The rider will duck to avoid that low branch.

_____

4. The sailor opened the hatch of the submarine.

_____

Name _____

63

Read the words and their meanings in each box. Write the words to finish the story. Write **1** or **2** in the box after each word to tell which meaning the word has in the sentence.

1. **play** —to take part in a game or sport 2. **play** —a story written to be acted on a stage	1. **stars** — bright spots of light in the night sky 2. **stars** — those with leading parts in a play
1. **rest** — sleep 2. **rest** — the part left over; remainder	1. **watch** —look at 2. **watch** —a small clock worn on the wrist

Anna looked again at the _____ ☐ on the table next to her bed. She was so excited she thought she'd never get any _____ ☐ . Tomorrow she would find out whether she was going to be one of the _____ ☐ in the school _____ ☐ . She had always dreamed of being an actress.

She'd spent the evening trying to take her mind off tomorrow. She had tried to _____ ☐ T.V. She had tried to _____ ☐ checkers with her sister.

She stared out her bedroom window at the _____ ☐ and thought. What would happen if she got the part? Would it change the _____ ☐ of her life? Would she someday be a famous actress? Finally, dreaming of stardom, she drifted off to sleep.

Name

Sometimes people use colorful "sayings" in their speech. Often, the words in a saying do not mean what they usually do. Instead, the words in a "saying" go together to mean something quite different from what the individual words mean. Underline the correct meaning for each "saying" below.

1. If you say, "It's raining cats and dogs," you do not mean that cats and dogs are falling from the sky. What do you mean?
   A. It is raining very hard.
   B. The drops of rain are very big.
   C. It is not raining very hard.

2. What do you think is really meant by, "She is as cool as a cucumber"?
   A. She is like a green vegetable.
   B. She does not let things bother her.
   C. Cucumbers are chilly.

3. "A drop in the bucket" does not mean that there is a drop of something in a bucket. What does it mean?
   A. A small amount of something.
   B. There is water in the bucket.
   C. Only a bucket could hold a drop of water.

4. "Tickled pink" does not mean that someone turned colors. What does it mean?
   A. Someone is delighted.
   B. Someone is laughing a lot.
   C. Someone is being tickled too much.

5. If you say that someone is "in the doghouse," you do not mean he or she is acting like a dog. What do you mean?
   A. Someone is in a small place.
   B. Someone is in trouble.
   C. Someone is acting strangely.

Name

A. The meanings of words often change when prefixes or suffixes are added. Add a prefix or suffix from the box to each word below to make a new word that has the definition shown.

Prefixes		Suffixes	
pre-	means before	**-less**	means without
un-	means not	**-est**	means most
re-	means again	**-ful**	means full of

1. _____plant — plant again

2. _____locked — not locked

3. _____heat — heated before

4. warm _____ — most warm

5. joy _____ — full of joy

6. hope _____ — without hope

B. Read the paragraphs below. Circle the prefix or suffix in each underlined story word. Think about the way the prefix or suffix has changed the meaning of the base word. Then write a definition for each underlined word.

It was a beautiful summer day for a baseball game. The sky was cloudless. I was almost unable to control my excitement. "Let's go to the game!" I shouted to Mom.

"It isn't until tomorrow," she called back. I was so unhappy. The rest of the day seemed endless.

1. _____

2. _____

3. _____

4. _____

Name _____

A. Changes in Word Meanings

Change the meanings of the words below by making another drawing.

1. I have the **ring**!

2. I want to be a **conductor**.

3. Today is a **fair** day.

B. Changes in Word Meanings
Inferring

The sentences give clues to the meanings of the underlined words. Write what you think each underlined word means.

1. I will give you a <u>ring</u> when I get home from school. If you don't hear from me, please call.   _____

2. At lunchtime there is usually a long <u>line</u> at the delicatessen.   _____

3. I can't find my other <u>sock</u> and shoe.   _____

4. The teacher calls the <u>roll</u> at the beginning of each school day.   _____

Name
_____

C. Ordering Objects

Look at the picture of the circus parade. Then complete 1 and 2.

1. Write the names of the animals from the shortest animal to the tallest animal.

   _____

2. Write the names of the animals in alphabetical order.

   _____

D. Anticipating Probabilities

Look again at the picture. Then write what will probably happen next.

1. The monkey will _____

   _____

2. The giraffe will _____

   _____

3. The elephant will _____

   _____

Name _____

Critical Thinking, Level C © 1993 Steck-Vaughn

Analyzing

Analyzing means seeing how parts fit together. What is happening in this picture? Is it easy for the child to blow the horn? What type of sound do you think the horn is making? Can the child make the horn sound differently? How do you know?

Circle the groups of words that are not complete sentences. Use the lines below to make sentences out of the groups of words you circled. The first one is done for you.

1. Our club has many new members.

2. (A person who cannot.)

3. Snookie, my pet snake.

4. Tina took a walk in the woods.

5. Climbed the ladder yesterday.

6. When Alice came to our school.

7. Where flowers are growing.

8. The day was bright and sunny.

9. A good show last night.

10. A fine friend to have.

2. A baby is a person who cannot go to school.

_____

_____

_____

_____

_____

_____

Name _____

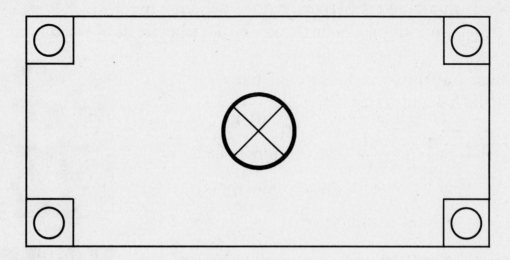

Choose inches or centimeters as your unit of measurement. Then check the two sets of directions below. Which set do you think is better? Explain your choice on the lines below.

A. 1. Draw a rectangle 5 units by 2 1/2 units.
   2. Find the center of the box and draw a circle.
   3. Put an X big enough to touch the sides in the center of the circle.
   4. Make a 1/2 square unit out of each corner of the rectangle.
   5. Put a small circle in each corner box. Do not make it touch the sides.

B. 1. Draw a rectangle.
   2. Put a circle in the middle of the box.
   3. Draw an X in the center of the circle.
   4. Make a box out of each corner.
   5. Put a circle in each of the boxes.

_____

_____

_____

_____

Name
_____

Read each numbered sentence. Find a sentence with a letter before it that tells the same thing. Write **X** on the line before that sentence.

1. The horses at the farm like to eat hay.

_____ a. Farm animals eat many things.

_____ b. Hay is what all farm animals eat.

_____ c. Hay is what the horses on the farm eat.

2. Ellen wished that her wagon could go faster.

_____ a. Ellen's wagon was too fast.

_____ b. Ellen's wagon needed to go faster.

_____ c. Ellen wished the wagon was not so slow.

3. Patty can read a story very well.

_____ a. Patty is a good reader.

_____ b. Patty likes to read.

_____ c. Patty reads all the time.

4. Juan finished his glass of juice.

_____ a. Juan likes juice.

_____ b. Juan put down the juice glass.

_____ c. Juan drank the juice.

Name

Critical Thinking, Level C © 1993 Steck-Vaughn

For each activity, put **X** before the **two** things you think are most important.

1. If you wash dishes, you need to know

_____ where the water heater is.

_____ where to put the clean dishes.

_____ where to find the soap.

2. To paint a picture, you need to know

_____ who painted the last picture.

_____ where the paint is kept.

_____ which paper and brush to use.

3. To play in a ball game, you need to know

_____ where the game will be played.

_____ where you can get a ball and a bat.

_____ what the score will be.

4. To use the library, you must know

_____ how many books are there.

_____ when the library is open.

_____ how to get to the library.

Name

A. Read each sentence below. Pick a
   word from the list that completes
   the sentence best. Write the word
   in the sentence. Then write the
   word on the correctly numbered
   line in the **Word Box.**

Word Box

1					
2					
3					
4					
5					
6					

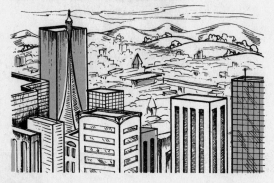

stores	better	crowds	police
houses	lights	best	building

1. In cities large _____ of people fill the streets.

2. There are many bright _____ in cities.

3. Some people think cities are _____ places to live than
   the suburbs.

4. Cities have large _____ and fire departments.

5. You may go shopping in many _____ .

6. There are many kinds of _____ to live in.

B. What word now appears in the darker squares of the **Word Box**?

   _____ Can you add anything about cities to the story?

   Write your own city story on another piece of paper.

Name _____

Critical Thinking, Level C © 1993 Steck-Vaughn

Words may tell about **concrete** things or **abstract** things. You can see, hear, touch, taste, or smell a concrete thing, such as a dog. You cannot see, hear, touch, taste, or smell an abstract thing, such as an idea. You can also easily draw a picture of a concrete thing. An abstract thing, like an idea, cannot always be pictured so clearly.

A. Put a check before each concrete thing below.

_____ house   _____ love   _____ pride   _____ baby

_____ thought   _____ camel   _____ honor   _____ pencil

_____ screen   _____ courage   _____ shirt   _____ plants

B. Read the sentences. Then circle the underlined words that are abstract.
   1. The small child had a <u>fear</u> of the dark.
   2. We will use paper <u>plates</u> for the picnic.
   3. The lovely <u>flower</u> also smells sweet.
   4. Paul showed <u>anger</u> when his sister broke his watch.
   5. I have a <u>notion</u> to take a walk.
   6. Marcia <u>said</u> she had a strange <u>feeling</u>.
   7. Dad's new <u>tie</u> is red, white, and blue.
   8. Most <u>parents</u> want <u>happiness</u> for their children.

C. Write a sentence using one of the words that you circled.

_____

_____

Name
_____

Abstract or Concrete

I. Some of the words below name things that people can make. Write **1** before them. Other words name parts of nature. You can see or hear or feel them. Write **2** before them. Still others name things that have to do with ideas or thinking. Write **3** before them.

_____ shoe	_____ flower	_____ love	_____ fog
_____ rain	_____ thunder	_____ ice cube	_____ popcorn
_____ table	_____ wind	_____ lamp	_____ stars
_____ idea	_____ box	_____ imagination	_____ dream

II. In box 1, write all the words you marked **1**. In box 2, write all the words you marked **2**. Then on the line before each word, write which letter fits that word. Write:

A—if you can see the thing named   **C**—if you can feel it
B—if you can hear the thing named   **D**—if you can smell it
                    E—if you can taste it

Some will have several letters. If a word you marked **3** fits one of the letters, think about the word again. You might want to mark it **1** or **2**.

1		**2**	
letters	words	letters	words
_____	_____	_____	_____
_____	_____	_____	_____
_____	_____	_____	_____
_____	_____	_____	_____
_____	_____	_____	_____
_____	_____	_____	_____

Name _____

Critical Thinking, Level C © 1993 Steck-Vaughn

A. Where would you do each of the things listed below? For example, where would you use rhyming words? Read the groups of words under **Where?** You might use rhyming words **in a play** or **in a poem**. Put **1** on the lines before **in a play** and **in a poem**. Match each of the eight numbers to a place. You may match some numbers to more than one place.

1. use rhyming words   5. play running games

2. bounce balls   6. write numbers

3. eat   7. paint pictures

4. fly in a plane   8. wear a costume

Where?

_____ a. in math class   _____ f. in the lunchroom

_____ b. in a play   _____ g. on an envelope

_____ c. in art class   _____ h. to a faraway place

_____ d. at a party   _____ i. in a poem

_____ e. in the gym   _____ j. on the playground

B. Write a sentence of your own to tell where you might do each of the following.

1. Tell about places where you could read. _____

_____

2. Tell about places where you could ride in a sled. _____

_____

3. Tell about places where you could sleep. _____

_____

Name

A. Read each sentence and question. Check the parts that make sense.

1. Your best friend is sick. When you visit your friend, which of these things would you take for your friend to use?

_____ books   _____ crayons

_____ tennis racket   _____ bicycle

_____ fishing pole   _____ radio

2. It is raining outside, and your new friend is coming to your house to play. What could you do?

_____ play kickball   _____ play checkers

_____ make model cars   _____ play baseball

_____ play cards   _____ go for a bike ride

3. Your baby brother is always getting into your things in your room. What could you do?

_____ close the door to your room   _____ throw your things away

_____ have your dog guard your door   _____ get another room

_____ place your things out of his reach   _____ play with your brother's toys

B. Imagine that you forgot your lunch money for school. Write three things you could do.

1. _____

2. _____

3. _____

Name _____

Critical Thinking, Level C © 1993 Steck-Vaughn

A story is made up of different parts. One very important part is called the **setting**. The setting tells where the story takes place. Look at the settings under each question. Circle the setting that goes with the other information given about the story.

1. Pretend that you want to write a story about the adventures of an alley cat. What would be a likely setting?

   a large city   a small farm   the city zoo

2. You are going to read a story about the life of a sailor. Where would you expect the story to take place?

   on a desert   in a swimming pool   in a boat

3. You are going to write a scary Halloween story. Which of the following places would be the best setting for the story?

   a barnyard   a haunted house   a fire station   your house

4. Imagine that you are writing an adventure story about a group of children. Which setting would you choose?

   a cave   a park   a barn   a beach

5. What would be a good setting for a story about a surprise birthday party?

   someone's basement   the yard   a boat

Name

Read the story and answer the questions which follow.

When Lola visited her aunt and uncle's farm, her favorite friend was a soft, furry little animal. Its mother would not feed it, so Lola fed it milk from a bottle.

One day the little creature strayed away from the rest of the flock. Lola searched for it for a long time. It finally made a tiny bleat and Lola heard it. She was able to lead it home by holding out a bottle of milk.

1. Where does the story take place?

_____

2. What kind of animal was Lola's favorite friend?

_____

3. Write a good title for this story.

_____

4. How would Lola's part in the story change if the animal were a tiger?

_____

5. How would the story change if Lola had not heard the tiny bleat?

_____

6. How would the story change if Lola's aunt and uncle told her not to go near the animals?

_____

Name _____

Critical Thinking, Level C © 1993 Steck-Vaughn

Number each story to show the correct story order. Put **1** before the first part. Put **2** before the middle part. Put **3** before the last part.

_____ Maria's older brother Juan worked with animals at the natural science center. Maria went to a pay phone and asked Juan to come right away to free the sea gull.

_____ She followed the sound to a big ball of wire. A sea gull was tangled in the wire. Maria tried to get close to the gull, but it only became more tangled.

_____ Maria was walking along the beach. Suddenly, she heard a loud cry.

_____

_____ Amy was surprised when her mother's best friend drove by! She and Amy put the bike into the trunk of the car. Later, Amy and her cousin fixed the tire.

_____ Amy wanted to visit her cousin. Mother said that Amy could go on her bicycle.

_____ Amy had a flat tire on the way. She started pushing the bicycle along.

_____

_____ He was in luck! The fish were really biting today. He caught so many fish that he could not carry them home.

_____ He kept six fish and gave the rest to other people on the beach.

_____ Jesse walked down to the beach with his fishing pole and bait. He hoped to catch a few fish for dinner.

Name

Each story below has a sentence or a group of words that does not belong. Underline the group of words that you would take out of each story.

1. Yesterday our class went on a picnic to the park. Everyone brought sack lunches. Jack does not like picnics. We sat under the trees and ate lunch. It was a nice day for a picnic.

2. A raccoon sometimes makes its home in a tree trunk. There are many kinds of trees, too. It sleeps in the tree trunk all day and hunts at night for mice and insects.

3. Students keep busy at school. They read, write, do math, and play. The library is on the first floor. They do many different things each day.

4. There are several things you should know about sentences. Sentences begin with a capital letter. They end with a period or other punctuation mark. Sentences also have a subject and a predicate. Some sentences are silly.

5. Helen and Rita stayed after school today to help the teacher. They cleaned erasers, washed the boards, and looked out the window. They might help again tomorrow.

6. Children wear warm clothes to play in the snow. They put on mittens and boots. They make snowballs and slide down hills on sleds. It is hard to drive on a snowy road.

7. Some people are tall and others are short. Some people look sad and others look happy. My dog looks sad. No two people are alike.

8. The work on a flower garden may begin in the fall. That's when bulbs are planted. In early spring the green plants peek through the ground. Robins begin to sing. Soon, tulips, daffodils, and irises are blooming in the garden.

Name _____

Critical Thinking, Level C © 1993 Steck-Vaughn

Each sentence below gives only two choices. If only two choices are possible, write **T** for true before the sentence. If you can think of more choices than the sentence gives you, put **F** for false.

Examples:	**F**	You are either at school or at home.
		(You might be at a store or another place.)
	T	Either you have freckles or you don't.

_____ 1. Fleas jump only onto dogs or cats.

_____ 2. Either you are alive, or you are not alive.

_____ 3. You are either hungry or full.

_____ 4. You are either playing or working.

_____ 5. You may either leave or stay here.

_____ 6. Vegetables are either green or yellow.

_____ 7. Either you tell the truth, or you tell lies.

_____ 8. Either you are moving, or you are staying still.

_____ 9. A glass is either empty or full.

_____ 10. The fan is either on or off.

_____ 11. Either you wear glasses, or you do not wear glasses.

_____ 12. You write with either your left hand or your right hand.

_____ 13. Your hair is either blonde or brown.

_____ 14. Your parent is either a mother or a father.

Name _____

For each sentence, there are really more choices than the ones that the sentence gives you. Rewrite the sentence so that it tells about other choices.

Example: A table can be either round or square.
A table can be round, square, rectangular, oblong, or many other shapes.

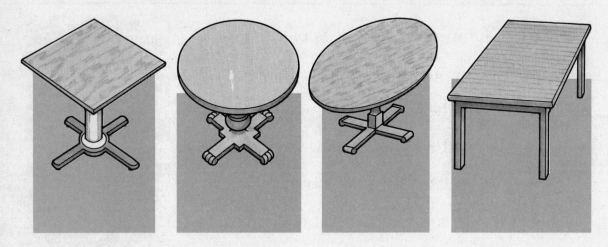

1. A ball must be either very large or very small. _____
_____

2. It will be very hot or very cold outside. _____
_____

3. All classrooms have twenty or twenty-five desks in them. _____
_____

4. Dogs are gray or brown. _____
_____

5. Garden tools are either rakes or hoes. _____
_____

Name _____

Critical Thinking, Level C © 1993 Steck-Vaughn

Sometimes if you are near the wrong thing or with a person who did something wrong, you may get into trouble. Put **X** before the sentences below which tell about places or happenings that could get you into trouble.

_____ 1. You are grocery shopping with your parents.

_____ 2. Your friend puts some comic books in your desk. You are not supposed to have them at school.

_____ 3. You are at the ballpark with your father and mother.

_____ 4. You and your friend find some rings. Later, you find out they were stolen.

_____ 5. You are at the circus with your uncle.

_____ 6. You are riding your bicycle where your parents said you could.

_____ 7. You did your school work all by yourself. But you have all the same wrong answers as your best friend.

_____ 8. You found a dime on the sidewalk.

_____ 9. You took some fruit from the refrigerator. Later, the refrigerator door was found standing open.

_____ 10. You are going outside to play.

_____ 11. You are standing next to a broken window.

_____ 12. You washed your bicycle. Later, your parents found that water was still pouring from the hose.

_____ 13. You often play with a group of children who have been seen breaking street lights.

_____ 14. There is broken glass in the kitchen, and you have been the only one at home today.

Name

Sometimes people want to persuade others to do something or think the way they do. In order to persuade, people sometimes slant their arguments in their favor. Read the pairs of sentences below. Write the one that slants or twists the facts.

1. You should see this movie because it will help you with your homework.
   This is a good movie if you are interested in the sea.

   _____

   _____

2. I need a new coat because the tear in mine can't be fixed.
   I would like a new coat.

   _____

   _____

3. This cereal is one thing you could have for breakfast.
   This cereal will give you all the energy you need.

   _____

   _____

4. We should eat our dessert first because it might melt if we wait.
   This dessert looks good, and I can't wait to eat it.

   _____

   _____

5. I would like to go first if you will let me.
   I should take the first turn at the game because I am the youngest.

   _____

   _____

Name _____

Critical Thinking, Level C © *1993 Steck-Vaughn*

A. —Judging Completeness

Look at the picture of an antique store window. Some of the items in the window have missing parts. In the sentences below, circle the word that tells what is needed to complete each item.

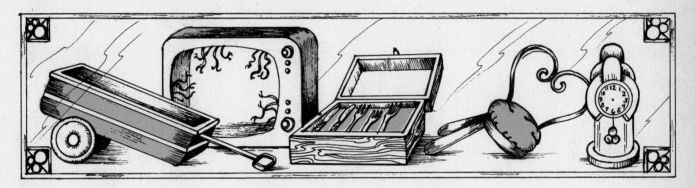

1. The clock needs   legs   hands   eyes.

2. The wagon needs   wheels   windows   doors.

3. The television needs a   handle   screen   frame.

4. The silverware chest is missing   forks   spoons   knives.

5. The chair needs   legs   wheels   sheets.

B. — Relevance of Information

Pretend that the items pictured above are complete. Write the name of the item you would use for each task.

1. to set the table for dinner _____

2. to sit at a desk to do homework _____

3. to take home many bags of groceries _____

4. to get to school on time _____

5. to get the latest news report _____

Name _____

C. Abstract or Concrete

Helena is going to spend the night at her friend Kay's house. Help Helena by writing on the lines in the duffel bag the things that she can pack.

pajamas	bathrobe
excitement	laughter
dreams	friendship
book	toothbrush
sleep	fun
comb	slippers
brush	eagerness

D. Story Logic

Read the sentences below to see if they make sense. The last sentence must make sense based on the information given in the first two sentences. Copy the last sentence if it makes sense.

1. Helena often spends the night at Kay's house. Kay sometimes spends the night at Helena's house. Helena and Kay are friends.

_____

2. Many people have dogs as pets. Sam has a pet. Sam has a dog.

_____

3. Many trees have fruit. The birch is a tree. The birch has fruit.

_____

Name _____

Synthesizing

Synthesizing means putting information together to come up with new ideas. Look at the picture. What is the girl doing? Is she the only one doing it? How do you know? Why do you think she is dressed this way? Do you think she is celebrating something? Why or why not?

Communicating Ideas

The International Morse Code is a famous way to send messages. It uses dots, dashes, and spaces. Can you read the coded message at the bottom? Look at the chart to find each symbol and the letter it stands for. Write each letter in a box under the symbol to make a sentence.

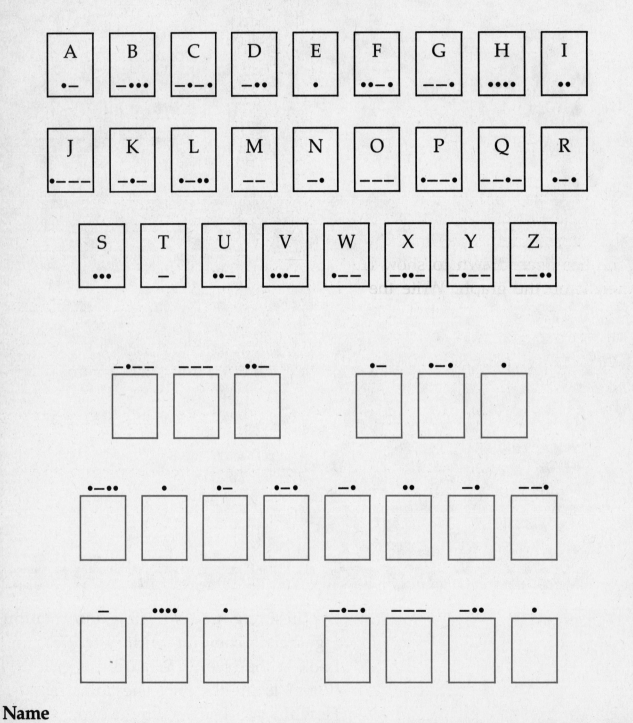

Critical Thinking, Level C © 1993 Steck-Vaughn

Name

Some children in the United States measured how tall they are:

Cindy is 44 inches tall.

Celia is 38 inches tall.

Marco is 42 inches tall.

Sally is 36 inches tall.

Jiro is 46 inches tall.

Rex is 48 inches tall.

Look at the graph below. Rex is the tallest child, so his name is written at the top. See that a line has been drawn to show his height on the graph. Write the name of the second tallest child on the second blank and draw a line to show the height. Go on until all the children's heights are shown.

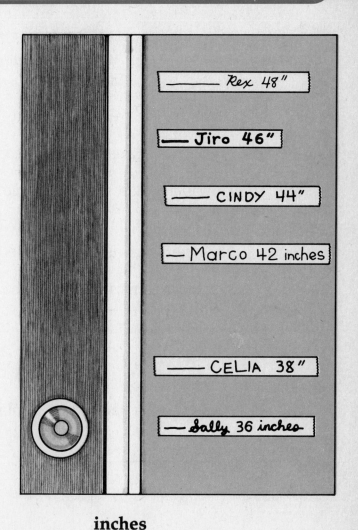

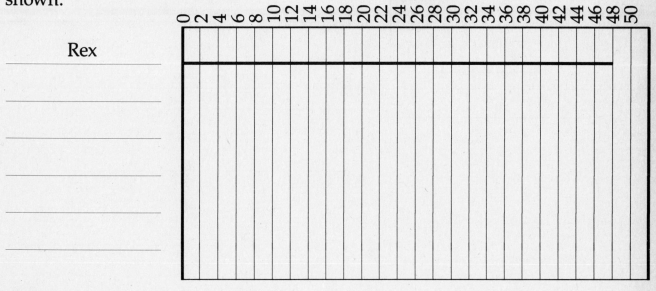

Rex

inches

Name

A. Signs communicate messages to drivers. Write the letter of each sign next to its message.

 a.
 d.

1. _____ No bicycles are allowed on this road.

2. _____ No U-turns are allowed here.

3. _____ This is a place where people cross the street.

 b.
 e.

4. _____ No right turn is allowed here.

5. _____ Warning! This is a railroad crossing.

6. _____ Warning! Deer cross the road here.

 c.
 f.

B. Think of two messages you could communicate using signs. Draw your signs below. Next to each sign, explain what it means and where you would put it.

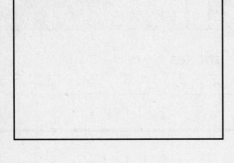

_____

_____

_____

_____

_____

_____

_____

_____

Name _____

A. Pretend that the art teacher has asked your class to make valentines. Underline any of the following things you could use.

tacks	scissors	paste	music
lace	crayons	ruler	white paper
red paper	clock	book	yarn

B. How should the valentines be made? Check the way you think is best.

_____ Each person should work alone.

_____ Two or three students should work together.

_____ The class should make one big valentine.

C. How much time should be used? Check your choice.

_____ Just one art period should be used.

_____ More than one art period should be used.

_____ An art period and some time at recess should be used.

_____ Whatever time is needed to get the job done should be used.

D. Do you think each of the three problems considered above is important?

_____ Why or why not? _____

_____

E. What else would you like to know about valentine making?

_____

_____

_____

Name _____

A. Nat was working on a wildlife display. He planned to make a plaster cast of some animal tracks he had seen. Check the things below that Nat might do.

_____ 1. call a friend on the telephone

_____ 2. talk to an adult about how to make a cast

_____ 3. feed his dog

_____ 4. collect materials

_____ 5. find out what the animal is

_____ 6. pour water on the tracks

B. These are the steps that Nat has to follow to make the plaster cast. **1** is next to the first thing that Nat should do. Number the rest of the steps in the order he should follow.

_____ Let the plaster get hard.

_____ Read and follow the directions to mix the plaster of paris.

_____ Pour the plaster of paris into the cardboard mold.

__1__ Place a ring of cardboard around the track to make a mold.

_____ Remove the cardboard mold when the plaster is hard.

_____ Turn the plaster cast over to see the raised animal track on the other side.

C. Once Nat has made his cast, he still needs to do some other things before his wildlife display is ready. Write at least two more things that you think Nat should do.

1. _____

2. _____

Name _____

Critical Thinking, Level C © 1993 Steck-Vaughn

Three reasons are given to explain why each thing happened. Can you think of another likely reason for each one? Write it on the line.

1. The class was noisy this morning.
   a. It might be that the teacher was out of the room.
   b. Perhaps some of the students were restless.
   c. It could be that they were playing a noisy game.

   d. Maybe _____

   _____

2. Our paintbrushes are not on the shelf where we keep them.
   a. It could be that another class borrowed them.
   b. Maybe they are in the sink to be cleaned.
   c. It might be that they were put away somewhere else.

   d. Perhaps _____

   _____

3. Mandy was late for her dentist appointment.
   a. It could be that Mandy was late on purpose because she doesn't like going to the dentist.
   b. Maybe the bus that Mandy took was late.
   c. Perhaps Mandy thought the appointment was at a later time.

   d. It might be that _____

   _____

4. Rudy renewed his book at the library.
   a. It could be that Rudy wanted to show the book to his teacher.
   b. Maybe Rudy wanted to reread the book.
   c. Perhaps Rudy needed to use the book to write a report.

   d. It might be that _____

Name _____

Study the picture. Then answer the questions.

1. What has happened in the picture?

_____

_____

2. Why has this happened?

_____

_____

3. What do you think will happen next?

_____

_____

Name

Critical Thinking, Level C © 1993 Steck-Vaughn

A. Read the story. Then check the sentence that gives the most likely reason for what happened.

Tim likes to cook. One day he made potato salad. As a dressing, he mixed sour cream and a little salt. Tim's family liked the salad. A few days later Tim made potato salad again. This time he used mayonnaise and salt as the dressing. Tim's family said the salad was too salty. The next time that Tim made potato salad dressing, he used yogurt and salt. Everyone said the dressing was fine.

Why was the second salad unsuccessful?

——— People have different tastes.

——— Tim's family doesn't like salt.

——— Mayonnaise already has salt in it.

——— The third salad was better.

B. How do you think Tim could make a salad dressing with mayonnaise that his family will like?

_____

_____

Name

Read the story. Then write the clues that the detective used to solve the mystery.

The Muffin Mystery

Someone ate the muffins that Mr. Selby left on the kitchen table. "They were right out of the oven," Mr. Selby told Detective Frank. "I left them here to cool."

"Hmmm," said Detective Frank as he looked around. "Whoever ate the muffins must be able to reach the table. Also, the thief did not eat all of the muffins, just little pecks from each one."

Detective Frank questioned the cat, the parrot, and the dog. These are the answers they gave.

"I don't like muffins," purred the cat.

Brushing a crumb from its feathers, the parrot said, "I don't know what you're talking about. But would you be kind enough to give me a nice cold drink of water? My mouth hurts."

"I do like muffins," said the dog. "But I can't reach the table top."

Detective Frank gave the parrot some water.

"Well, who ate my muffins?" asked Mr. Selby.

"It was this naughty parrot, I'm afraid!" answered Detective Frank.

Write 4 clues that helped Detective Frank.

_____

_____

_____

_____

Name

monkey   turtle   pig

dog   kitten   mouse

The children in Cindy's class are having a pet parade. They want to give prizes to the different animals. You are the judge.

1. Which animal would you choose as the most unusual?

_____ Why? _____

2. Which animal would you choose as the easiest to care for?

_____ Why? _____

3. Which animal would you choose as the most helpful to its owner?

_____ Why? _____

4. Which animal would you choose as the best at learning things?

_____ Why? _____

Name _____

Read each sentence. Choose an ending below that gives a reason for what happened. Write the letter of the ending on the line before the sentence.

_____ 1. Some workers were digging a large hole for a basement. They used picks to loosen the dirt, shovels to dig it up, and wheelbarrows to move it away. They would have finished sooner

_____ 2. A man was digging up his driveway with a pick. He was using a pick

_____ 3. My father needs to break up some huge rocks. He has decided to call someone with special tools

_____ 4. A factory owner has to move some big machines to a new plant. The owner called the railroad office

_____ 5. Mrs. Pine wants a new fireplace. She has decided to call a carpenter. Mrs. Maple thinks that Mrs. Pine is wrong

Reasons

A. since a freight car is big and strong enough to carry them.
B. because a bricklayer puts in the bricks for a fireplace.
C. since a rock crusher can do the job faster and easier.
D. because he did not have a jackhammer.
E. if they had used a tractor with a loader.

Name

Critical Thinking, Level C © 1993 Steck-Vaughn

Read each story. Then check the sentence under it that gives the best conclusion.

1. It was a crisp fall day. Mr. Larch drove slowly so nothing would fall off his truck. Anyway, he had to stop often to make pickups. At each stop Mr. Larch put on his gloves, got out, and threw big bags onto his truck. Almost all the leaves were off the trees and off the lawns, Mr. Larch noted. It would be a busy day.

   _____ Mr. Larch is picking up people's laundry.

   _____ Mr. Larch is collecting bags of leaves.

   _____ Mr. Larch is gathering sacks of mail.

2. Steve washed his finger in the sink. Then he found a bandage and put it on. Holding his finger carefully, Steve went back to his desk, took out a new sheet of paper, and began to write.

   _____ Steve cut his finger on a piece of paper.

   _____ Steve cut his finger on the sink.

   _____ Steve cut his finger on his desk.

3. Marie looked around the airport helplessly. She asked some people for directions but could not really understand what they said. Marie saw a sign, but she wasn't sure what it meant, either. Finally, Marie took a small book out of her bag and hunted through it.

   _____ Marie was a child who had lost her mother in an airport.

   _____ The airport was too noisy for Marie to understand anything.

   _____ Marie was in a foreign country and did not speak the language there.

Name _____

Read the story. Then answer the questions.

Usually, Wendy liked to run errands for her mother. She would put on her roller skates and go to the mailbox on the corner or the fruit stand down the street. Sometimes she rolled along to pick up the newspaper or to buy something at the grocery. When she had a lot to carry, Wendy took along the wagon. Wendy loved being on roller skates, so it didn't matter what her mother asked her to do or when it had to be done.

However, this summer Wendy's little brother Jimmy was old enough to talk and walk. Whenever he heard their mother ask Wendy to go on an errand, he said, "Me too." At first everyone thought it was cute and no one paid much attention to his demands. But as the days went by, Jimmy became **more** demanding.

"If you walk slowly, Jimmy can go with you," said Wendy's father.

Wendy was upset. Running errands was fun only because she did them on roller skates.

Wendy had trouble sleeping that night. "I wonder if Jimmy is old enough to skate," Wendy thought to herself. "Or maybe I can carry him. What will I do . . .?"

1. What do you think Wendy will do?

_____

_____

2. Why do you think Wendy will do that?

_____

_____

Name

Critical Thinking, Level C © 1993 Steck-Vaughn

Sometimes old or worn-out things can be used in new ways. Write the name of the old item under the new way to use it. See if you can think of some more uses for these old things.

a car that won't run   newspapers   old shoes
empty plastic bottles   torn shirts   old greeting cards

New Ways to Use Old Things

1. You could use the parts to make a scooter.

_____

2. You could use them to store liquids.

_____

3. You could make papier-mâché out of them.

_____

4. You could cut out the decorations and make new ones of your own.

_____

5. You could dust the furniture with them.

_____

6. You could use the tongue for a bookmark.

_____

Name _____

103

Here are some common things that could be used in many different ways. Put on your thinking cap. Write as many different uses for each thing as you can. Remember, you can do anything you want to with the objects. For example, you could cut or paste or fold them.

1.

ball of yarn

_____

_____

_____

2.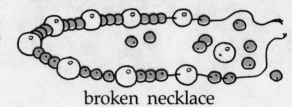

broken necklace

_____

_____

_____

3.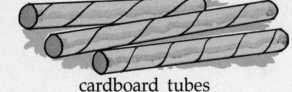

cardboard tubes

_____

_____

_____

4.

clothespins

_____

_____

_____

5.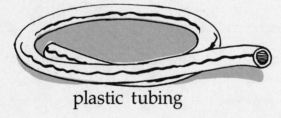

plastic tubing

_____

_____

_____

6.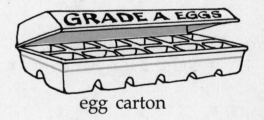

egg carton

_____

_____

_____

Name _____

Critical Thinking, Level C © 1993 Steck-Vaughn

Karen has just moved to a new city. She will go to Lincoln School for the first time on Monday morning. She does not know any of the students there. Karen is afraid of meeting so many new people. Maybe the students at Lincoln School can help Karen feel better about her first day there.

A. Here is a list of things the students might do on Karen's first day at Lincoln School. Put **X** before each sentence that tells how Karen would like to be treated.

_____ 1. Give Karen some wrong facts about the school.

_____ 2. Try to get in line ahead of her.

_____ 3. Show Karen how to find her way around the school.

_____ 4. Carefully answer the questions she asks.

_____ 5. Do not sit beside her at lunch.

_____ 6. Let Karen take part in the games they are playing.

_____ 7. Talk to Karen in a friendly way.

B. Use the lines below to tell three more ways to help Karen.

1. _____

_____

2. _____

_____

3. _____

_____

Name _____

⟨ Proposing Alternatives ⟩

When you have a problem, you often think of different ways to solve it. If your car won't start, you ride with a friend or take a bus. Suppose the problems below happened to you. Write a sentence below each problem to tell what you might do.

1. There is a leak in the town's water system. Everyone's water has been shut off. How can you get water for drinking, cooking, and bathing?

   _____

   _____

2. Your apartment building does not have any yard. You often play ball in the vacant lot next door. Today some workers came to the lot to put up a big building. Now where will you play ball?

   _____

   _____

3. A bad storm knocked out the electric power in your city. It will take two days to make all the repairs. How can you see in your house after dark?

   _____

   _____

4. You lost your wallet this week. In it was the money you had saved to buy your sister a birthday present. How will you get a gift for her now?

   _____

   _____

Name

_____

Critical Thinking, Level C © 1993 Steck-Vaughn

A. Communicating Ideas

The Mayans lived many hundreds of years ago. The symbol on the right is a number from their writing system. Each bar stands for **5**. Each dot stands for **1**. So this symbol means **12**. The chart below should show symbols for the numbers **1** to **20**. Use Mayan symbols to fill in the missing numbers.

•	• •		• • • •
——		• • ——	
		• ══	
• • • ══	• • • • ══		• ═══
		• • • • ═══	

B. Planning Projects

Next to each activity on the left, write the letters of the things you need to do that activity.

_____ 1. write in code

_____ 2. wash your hands

_____ 3. sew a seam

_____ 4. make bread

a. needle   e. thread

b. soap   f. recipe

c. paper   g. water

d. pencil   h. flour

Name _____

C. Developing Conclusions

At the Souvenir Shop, only one salesperson is waiting on customers. Where is that person? Read each clue. Find the department mentioned. Put an **X** on it on the map. Which one is left? You've solved the mystery!

1. The salesperson in Jewelry is out sick.
2. The salesperson in T-Shirts is on the phone.
3. The clerks in Hats and Hankies are having a meeting.
4. Everyone in Posters and Maps is taking a break.

The salesperson is in _____.

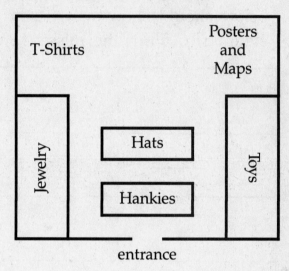

D. Proposing Alternatives

For each item write another use.

1. map   hang it on a wall

_____

2. bicycle   ride it to school

_____

3. computer   play a game

_____

4. trunk   pack clothes

_____

Name _____

Evaluating

Evaluating means making a judgment or decision about something. Look at the picture. Does the girl like birds? How can you tell? Do you think this bird is tame? Why or why not? Does a bird make a good pet? Would you like to have one? Why or why not?

Read each statement and the words below it. If the statement is true for all of the words, write **yes** on the line. If the statement is not true for some words, write **no** on the line. Put **X** on the words that make the statement wrong.

_____ 1. The pairs of words are opposites.
dark—light   yes—no   big—large

_____ 2. All of these words rhyme.
bark   mark   park   lack   dark

_____ 3. Each word has three syllables.
family   bicycle   animal   tomorrow

_____ 4. The words in each pair sound the same.
buy—bye   bear—bare   too—two   through—threw

_____ 5. All of the words end with the same two consonants.
pink   rink   sing   think   sink

_____ 6. The words in each pair mean about the same.
noisy—loud   circle—ring   touch—feel

_____ 7. These words have three letters that are the same.
dear   heart   wear   beard   earth

_____ 8. These words have the same vowel sound.
load   pole   know   toe   bone

_____ 9. Since these words end in **s**, they are all plurals.
dogs   rugs   this   bus   lips

_____ 10. These words have the same vowel sound.
torn   born   morn   rock   worn

_____ 11. These words are in alphabetical order.
stamp   twin   work   your   zone

Name _____

Read the sentences with numbers before them. Find a statement with a letter before it which proves that the numbered statement is not always true. Connect them with a line.

1. Everyone should drink three glasses of milk each day.

2. All four-legged animals have soft fur.

3. Dogs are friendly animals.

4. No one likes Harry.

5. Animals that live in the water are called fish.

6. All birds can fly.

7. Boys are taller than girls.

8. It is always quiet in the country.

9. All sharks are dangerous.

10. Hot water is the best way to clean clothes.

a. Porpoises and whales are mammals that live in the water.

b. Dogs who are mistreated get cross and mean.

c. Harry's parents and neighbors think he is a fine fellow.

d. Porcupines have sharp quills.

e. Milk makes some people get a rash.

f. The ostrich cannot use its small wings to fly.

g. You should clean some spots with cold water.

h. Jenny is taller than John.

i. Farm animals make a lot of noise when they are hungry.

j. Whale sharks do not harm people.

Name

Each of these sentences states something that is not always true. Write a sentence to prove that the statement is not always true.

> **Example:** In a city, everyone lives in an apartment building.
>
> Esmerita lives in a house.

1. People who work always go to an office.

_____

2. All doctors wear eyeglasses.

_____

3. Everyone who goes to the beach knows how to swim.

_____

4. All cats are pets.

_____

5. Outdoor games are always played with a ball.

_____

6. All teachers are women.

_____

7. Everyone who goes to school rides a bus.

_____

8. All boats have motors.

_____

Name _____

kitten   fish   parakeet

dog   pony

A. Answer these questions about the pets above.

1. Which is the most quiet? _____

2. Which one can guard your house? _____

3. Which one can chirp merrily? _____

4. Which could you **not** play with? _____

5. Which would you **not** keep in your house? _____

6. Which is the easiest to take on a trip? _____

B. What things do you think are most important to keep in mind in choosing a pet?

_____

_____

Name
_____

A. Imagine that you are buying books for each of the people described below. Use what you read about each person to choose the books they would enjoy most. Write the letters of the best book choices before each name.

a.    b.    c.    d.

e.    f.    g.

1. _____ Alex—He is interested in animals. He enjoys working at his mom's pet store. He has a big aquarium at home. He likes to read about real and imaginary animals.

2. _____ Sara—She loves science. She likes to build things, try to figure out how things work, and solve all kinds of mysteries. She would like to be an inventor when she grows up.

B. What things do you keep in mind when you choose a book for

yourself? _____

_____

Decide which book shown above you might enjoy. Write its title and give two reasons for your choice.

_____

_____

Name

When you read or listen, ask yourself if what is written or said makes sense. Sometimes people say one thing and then another that is different. When this happens, it is hard to know what they really mean.

Read these paragraphs. Find two sentences in each that **contradict**, or say the opposite thing. Underline these sentences.

1. Elisha Otis invented the elevator in 1852. With his invention people could go from floor to floor in a building without climbing stairs. This invention made it possible for people to build tall skyscrapers. Thank you, Mr. Otis, for inventing the escalator.

2. Pioneers worked hard from morning to night. They hunted, plowed the land, and made their own clothes. They usually sat around and played games. They also made their own tools, built their homes, and wove their own cloth.

3. Many people remember Ben Franklin because he did an experiment with a kite and lightning. Ben Franklin is known for many other things, too. He started a hospital, a college, and a library. He also ran a print shop. Ben Franklin never did any scientific work, however.

4. The way a clown's face is painted is very important. Each clown's face is different from all the other clowns. When you go to the circus, all the clowns look alike.

5. Schools in India are not like schools here. Many boys and girls in India do not go to school. Instead of going to school, they stay at home and help with the work. Children in India who do not go to school get to play all day.

6. The Wright brothers were interested in flying. They read books about flying and drew pictures of things that might fly. They thought flying was boring. In 1900 they built a glider and tried to fly it.

Name _____

Sometimes when people speak or write, they are not exact. This makes it hard to understand just what they mean. You cannot make good judgments about things if you do not know what is really meant.

Read the paragraph. Find five examples of a word or words that are not exact. Underline these words. Then rewrite the paragraph using more exact words for those that you underlined.

The new restaurant was sort of pretty. The menu was not bad and the food was nice. The service was okay, too. We kind of liked it.

_____

_____

_____

_____

_____

_____

Name

When you judge something, you come to a conclusion about it. It is important that your conclusions make sense. When you make a conclusion, base it on the facts that are given.

Read the two paragraphs. Underline the concluding sentence in each paragraph. Then circle the conclusion that does not follow the facts given.

> George looked at many bikes before he decided which one to buy. When George was getting a new radio, he read about the different kinds on the market. George decided on his new sunglasses after trying on several pairs. George is a careful shopper.

> George looked at many bikes before he decided which one to buy. When George was getting a new radio, he read about the different kinds on the market. George decided on his new sunglasses after trying on several pairs. George spends his money carelessly.

Reread the sentence you circled. Write why the conclusion does not make sense.

_____

_____

_____

Name _____

Judging Accuracy

When you write a report, you get information from different places or sources. It is important to make good choices about the sources that you use.

Read the paragraph below. Then fill in each blank with one of the sources given in the box. Choose the best source for each sentence.

dictionary	encyclopedia	map	song
chart	poem	radio	girl from Egypt

The _____ shows that Egypt is in Africa. The capital of Egypt is Cairo. The _____ says that it is pronounced **kī´ rō**. I read in the _____ that most people in Egypt are farmers. I also learned that the Nile River is very important to Egypt. It provides most of the country's water. Just this morning on the _____ there was a report about how many people live along the Nile. I would like to meet a _____ to find out more about life in Egypt.

Name _____

There are often many ways to do something. Some ways are better than others. It is a good idea to stop and think about all the possibilities before you decide.

Each sentence tells about what someone wants to do. The three sentences that follow give ways it could be done. Underline the sentence that you think tells the best way.

1. Mr. Blake wants to sell his car.
   a. He could put a sign in his apartment window.
   b. He could run an ad in the newspaper.
   c. He could put a note on the bulletin board in the library.

2. Leon wants to win the costume contest.
   a. He could make a costume that no one else has thought of.
   b. He could wear his costume from last year.
   c. He could wear the costume he wore in the school play.

3. Rita wants to get extra sleep so she will have more energy for playing soccer.
   a. She could sleep later in the morning.
   b. She could take naps after school.
   c. She could go to bed earlier at night.

4. Honey wants to surprise her dad with a great birthday gift.
   a. She could ask him what he wants.
   b. She could watch and listen to find out what he might need or like.
   c. She could ask the clerk in the store for help.

Name _____

There are often many ways to do something. Some ways are better than others. It is a good idea to stop and think about all the possibilities before you decide.

Read the paragraphs. Each tells about what someone wants to do. Decide what you think is the best way to solve the problem. Write your idea on the lines.

1.   Rufus has an aunt in another city who is ill. Rufus would like his aunt to know that he is thinking of her. What should Rufus do?

   _____

   _____

   _____

2.   Mei Ling started in a new school one week ago. She doesn't know her classmates very well yet. Today is Mei Ling's birthday. How should she celebrate it?

   _____

   _____

   _____

3.   Paul sometimes baby-sits for a neighbor's son. The little boy does not always obey Paul. What should Paul do?

   _____

   _____

   _____

Critical Thinking, Level C © 1993 Steck-Vaughn

Name _____

When you decide to do something, you want to do it correctly. Often you can follow rules or guidelines that tell you how something should be done.

Read the guidelines that tell how to make something. Then read the paragraph that Raoul wrote.

- List the materials you need.
- Tell things in order.
- Use time words such as **first, next, then**, and **last**.

First, scoop up a large pile of sand with your hands. Next, get pails of water and wet the sand down so you can work with it. Then, begin molding the sand into the shape you want. You may need to add more sand and water as you work. The last thing you do is put the finishing touches on your sculpture. Use a plastic knife or spoon to carve the features.

1. What did Raoul leave out in his directions?

_____

2. Write the part of the directions that Raoul left out.

_____

_____

_____

Name

121

Whatever it is that you do, you want to do in the right or correct way. Often, there are rules or guidelines for doing certain things.

Read the guidelines for writing a poem. Then read the poem to see if it follows the guidelines.

- The poem should be 6 lines long.
- The first and second lines should rhyme, the third and fourth lines should rhyme, and the fifth and sixth lines should rhyme.
- The poem should be about giving advice.

I try to be kind and nice
When someone asks for advice.
I tell them what I think or know;
What to do or how to go.
In turn, my friends help me, too,
When I'm not sure what to do.

Now it's your turn. Write a poem of your own. Follow the guidelines given above.

_____

_____

_____

_____

_____

_____

Name _____

A. Listed below are some things you can do. Some of them are helpful and fair. Put **H** in front of these. Some of the statements describe unfair acts or acts that would not be helpful. Put **X** in front of those acts.

_____ 1. You could help your parents clean the house.

_____ 2. You could leave your toys all over the room.

_____ 3. You could always fight to be the first batter in the ball game.

_____ 4. You could ask your new neighbor to play with you and your friends.

_____ 5. You could pick up the coat on the floor, even though it is not yours.

_____ 6. You could take a big handful of popcorn when there is not enough for everyone.

B. Choose one of the two ways to finish the sentences below. Put **X** before the ending that tells what you would do.

1. You saw Lois drop some paper in the park. You should

_____ mind your own business.

_____ remind Lois not to litter.

2. You bought a whistle that does not work. You should

_____ go back to the store and trade it for another whistle.

_____ throw it away and buy a new one.

3. You saw Dean push a younger boy down on the playground. You should

_____ push Dean down.

_____ try to help the younger boy.

Name _____

Read the story. Then write answers to the questions.

Jonathan didn't know what he was going to do. His best friends, Mike and Chris, had just left on vacation for the rest of the summer. The next two months were going to be very lonely!

After a few days, Jonathan started playing with Brian. Brian lived down the block. Jonathan hadn't played with Brian before because Mike and Chris didn't like Brian. As the summer days sped by, the two boys became the best of friends. They did everything together.

Jonathan and Brian were in the middle of an exciting game near the summer's end. The doorbell rang, and there stood Mike and Chris. They rushed in, full of stories about their summer. But they stopped short when they saw Brian. "What's he doing here?" whispered Mike. "Tell him to go home."

1. What are three things Jonathan might do?

a. _____

_____

b. _____

_____

c. _____

_____

2. What do you think Jonathan should do? Why?

_____

_____

_____

Name

Critical Thinking, Level C © 1993 Steck-Vaughn

Read the sentences. Try to put yourself in the place of the characters. How do they feel? Circle the word that best describes the feeling.

1. Mom settled back in her chair, gave a happy sigh, and opened her book.
   a. content   b. nervous   c. amused

2. As night fell, the woods seemed to close in on us. Strange noises filled the air, and I was sure that something lurked behind every tree or bush.
   a. pleasant   b. scary   c. calm

3. The young man who had been sick won the prize for his story.
   a. disturbed   b. pleased   c. unhappy

4. The girl who did the high-wire circus act slipped, started falling, and then quickly got back on the wire.
   a. excited   b. worried   c. sad

5. Carl gave Martin a hard kick. Martin landed on the ice. He got a cut on his head.
   a. glad   b. sorry   c. angry

6. Pete slammed the book down on his desk. His face was red.
   a. happy   b. angry   c. sad

7. The blazing sun burned my skin until it was too sore to touch. I groaned.
   a. proud   b. unhappy   c. pleasant

8. The glowing fire kept us warm while we popped corn and toasted marshmallows. Outside, the snowflakes danced at the windows.
   a. restless   b. lonely   c. cozy

Name

Read the paragraph. Then answer the questions.

Amy saw that the big easy chair was empty. She smiled to herself, then went and got her potholder loom and the colored loops that went with it. She turned on the lamp against the late afternoon darkness and found her favorite music station on the radio. Then Amy sank into the comfortable chair with a sigh. Outside the storm raged. The rain beat against the windows, but Amy didn't mind. Her foot tapped to the soft music as she wove a pretty potholder on her loom.

1. In this story how does Amy feel?

   _____

   _____

2. How would you describe the place where the story takes place?

   _____

   _____

   _____

   _____

3. What is happening outside the place where Amy is?

   _____

   _____

   _____

   _____

Critical Thinking, Level C © 1993 Steck-Vaughn

Name

126

A. Testing Generalizations

Read each statement and the words which follow it. If the statement is true, write **true** on the line. If the statement is not true about all the items, write **not true**.

1. _____ These items can all be found in a bedroom.
   bathtub bed chest rug pillow
2. _____ These items can all be read.
   book magazine newspaper letter sign
3. _____ These animals all live in the water.
   shark lobster frog seahorse seal
4. _____ These are different kinds of flowers.
   rose violet tulip banana daisy
5. _____ You can climb all of these things.
   ladder floor stairs rope mountain

B. Developing Criteria

Fill in the chart to find out who is who. Then write the name of each boy under his picture.

Fred	Ned
Ed	Ted

Ned and Ted have dark eyes.
Ed, Ned, and Fred have black hair.
Ted and Fred wear glasses.

Name _____

C. — Judging Accuracy

Read the two paragraphs. Underline the conclusion in each paragraph. Circle the conclusion that does not make sense.

1. Andy struck out for the third time today. He angrily threw the bat on the ground. Then he picked up his glove and ran off toward home. Andy was a good sport.

2. Meg took Butter, her golden retriever, for his second walk of the day. When they got home she fed him, brushed his coat, and tried again to teach him to stay at her command. Meg is a caring pet owner.

D. — Identifying Values

Read the story. Then answer the questions.

Lena was disappointed! She'd saved all summer for new gym shoes. She was sure they'd help her make the basketball team. But today she found that the price had gone up. She needed just fifty cents more!

Lena looked ahead and saw a man picking up change from the sidewalk. The man had dropped it while he was feeding a parking meter. As the man straightened up and began walking away, Lena noticed two quarters the man hadn't picked up.

1. What things might Lena do? _____

_____

_____

2. What do you think Lena should do? Why? _____

_____

_____

Name _____

Critical Thinking, Level C © 1993 Steck-Vaughn

128